How to End Exam Anxiety

The Ultimate Approach for Parents, Teachers & Students

Fran Burke, M.Ed.

Copyright © 2016 by Fran Burke

No part of this publication may be reproduced or transmitted in any form, or by electronic or mechanical means, including any information storage or retrieval system, without permission in writing from the publisher.

ISBN: 978-1-77277-077-3

Published by
10-10-10 Publishing
Markham, Ontario
CANADA

For my protection and yours, I want you to know the following:

The information contained this book, including ideas, suggestions, techniques, and other materials, is educational in nature and is provided only as general information and is not medical or psychological advice.

Transmission of the information in this book is not intended to create (and receipt does not constitute) a client-practitioner relationship or any other type of professional relationship between the reader and Fran Burke and should not be used as medical, psychological, coaching, or other professional advice of any kind or nature. Please consult your licensed health care provider for any issues.

I dedicate this book to my parents who, by example, inspired me to learn, to grow and to be open to change and to the Universe to guide my way.

Testimonials

Most people will recall the anxiety they have experienced in taking exams. Finally a book that acknowledges this issue and gives a comprehensive solution of short term and long term strategies to help students maximize their performance and success. Best of all, Fran incorporates the latest research on the brain and learning with practical strategies from Brain Gym®, EFT, Growth Mind Set, Mind Mapping and more. Great for all students and the teachers and parents that support them.

Emil Boychuk
Chair of the Association of Career Educators
Former Guidance Instructional Leader at the Toronto District School Board

After reading this book I was delighted by the content and the depth that really applies to everyone who is facing a challenge. I liked that Fran included Dr. Carol Dweck's, resilience or "growth mindset". The whole idea of effort and persistence is essential to everyone who wants to succeed. Fran did a good

Fran Burke, M.Ed.

job on explaining stress, Brain Gym® and Emotional Freedom Techniques. But what I really found helpful was the depth Fran went into on goal setting, study habits, exam-taking skills and especially self-motivation and taking care of one's self. What Fran included applied aptly also to optimal living --- for success, joy and good relationships. It reminded me of what works best in my own life --- and I think what Fran has written applies, not only to students and teachers, but as I said earlier, anyone who is facing a challenge or just wants some guidelines to live more fully.

This book is important and should be a read for every teacher and parent at the least. I like that it is short --- that is what people are able to read these days with their hectic schedules --- and everyone can use the Brain Gym® and EFT.

Carla Hannaford, Ph.D.
Biologist/Author/International Consultant

A thorough reading of 'How to End Exam Anxiety, the Ultimate Approach for Parents, Teachers and Students' will change the course of a student's life. It gives them, at their fingertips, all the practical skills and knowledge to take control of their exam anxiety – and their life!

Fran Burke's experience as a teacher and guidance counselor combines powerfully with her passion for the brain body connection. She brings an integrated head and heart perspective to this important issue that is rampant and largely ignored in our educational institutions.

This book matters. It matters that students, teachers, parents, counsellors and administrators understand that exam anxiety can be resolved with easily learned, scientifically supported self-help strategies. They need to know that exam anxiety does not 'go away' after the exam is over. It persists in the student's emotional, cognitive and physical experience, negatively impacting their self-image and their willingness and ability to pursue their goals and dreams.

Fran Burke's work supports an evolutionary perspective on how the body and emotions impact the learning process. Knowing and practicing the skills she teaches empowers us to expand both our performance and our happiness.

Nancy Forrester
MBA, Clinical Member Ontario Society of Psychotherapists, Accredited Master EFT Trainer of Trainers (AAMET International)
Founder and CEO, National Emotional Freedom Techniques Training Institute (NeftTI.com)

Fran Burke, M.Ed.

As a University graduate and a mother of two, I understand the importance of academic success and examination skills. Similar to building wealth (my area of expertise), taking exams is a learnable skill. One of the fastest ways for people (adults and children) to build their "exam muscle" is through having the right conversations with expert mentors. Fran Burke is that expert mentor.

Fran understands the need to address exam anxiety for the everyday student. Based on solid research, she offers compelling approaches to manage it. She takes the mystery out of exam anxiety and shows how to counter the involuntary physical and mental response to the stress of exams with voluntary thought and action.

Loral Langemeier
Bestselling Author, Speaker and Wealth Coach

Acknowledgements

I would like to express my gratitude to the following individuals:

My husband, Oscar R. Rivero for his unfailing support, encouragement and patience throughout the writing of this book and during the many hours of specialized training that preceded it and which contributed hugely to the content and authority with which the book is written.

Ka'ren Feder who planted the seed for the writing of this book having noticed that my teaching/counselling experience and extensive training in health and wellness modalities were perfect for helping students end exam anxiety.

I would like to thank all those who helped with the process of getting the book written, edited and published. Raymond Aaron for the 10-10-10 Program™. Without it and the dedication of his staff, this book would not have been written. Clayton Bye for his contribution to the content and editing of the manuscript. Gerald McManus for his valued ideas and encouragement. Daisy Fae Auer for her expert skill as a photographer. Kari Coady, Executive Director of Brain Gym® International for reviewing and commenting on the Brain Gym® portion of this

Fran Burke, M.Ed.

book. My teacher, Nancy Forrester of the National EFT Training Institute (NeftTI) for her encouragement and support in writing the EFT section of this book.

I would like to thank those from whom I have learned so much and whose knowledge and insights I have the privilege to share. Carla Hannaford for the breadth and depth of her work revealing the role that the body plays in brain development and learning and foundational to the content of this book. Gary Craig who created Emotional Freedom Techniques and its revolutionary and transforming role in the area of healing and well-being. Paul and Gail Dennison who gifted the world with Brain Gym®, a branch of Educational Kinesiology. It is ground breaking in the field of education and personal empowerment and well-being.

To my teachers and trainers for all their hours of training. Nancy Forrester of the National EFT Institute (NeftTI) in the field of Emotional Freedom Techniques and Sher Smith of Realizing Your Potential in the fields of Brain Gym®, Touch for Health and Polarity Therapy. I am eternally grateful.

Last but not least, to my husband's two daughters whom I love as my own, Jamina Wendland and Melissa Rivero, and my sister-in-law, Catherine Burke for their much appreciated encouragement.

I beg forgiveness to those whom I may have overlooked mentioning and wish to thank in spite of such an omission.

Contents

Foreword	xiii
Preface	xvii
For the Student	xxv
For Parents/Caregivers	xxix
For Teachers	xxxiii
About the Author	xxxix

UNIT ONE: About Exam Anxiety	**1**
Chapter 1: Aspects of Exam Anxiety	3
Chapter 2: Exam Anxiety and the Survival Response	15
Chapter 3: Indicators of Exam Anxiety	25
Chapter 4: Am I Alone	37
UNIT TWO: Short-Term Solutions for Exam Anxiety	**47**
Chapter 5: Calm Your Anxiety with Brain Gym®	49
Chapter 6: Calm Your Anxiety with EFT	73
UNIT THREE: Long-Term Solutions	**89**
Chapter 7: Growth Mindset	91
Chapter 8: Goal Setting	99
Chapter 9: Study Habits, Learning Methods and Exam-Taking Skills	109

Chapter 10: Self-Care 141
Appendix 159
Bibliography 169

FOREWORD

Are you a student who experiences exam anxiety or a parent with a child who experiences it? Or are you a teacher who recognizes that your students have exam anxiety? If you have picked up this book, your answer must be "yes". You are most likely looking for solutions to this anxiety. If you are a student, your grades may be suffering and you may be unable to control the unpleasant physical and emotional affects brought on by such anxiety. As a parent, you may feel helpless as you watch your child exhibit anxious behaviors in face of exams, and have no way to help. As a teacher, you may see your students displaying any number of anxious behaviors before an exam and wish you could do something to make a difference.

I have always believed that the first step with any challenge is always to take ownership of the challenge you face. In this case it would be a challenge with your own exam anxiety, or a challenge a parent or teacher faces by helping someone who does experience it. You may ignore it, hoping it will go away if it is ignored long enough. I have made it my life's mission through my writings and The Monthly Mentor® Program to teach you to meet challenges head on. This means facing the

Fran Burke, M.Ed.

challenges and using a step-by-step guide as a solution. One way to do this is to recognize the mental and emotional resistance to the challenge. The other is to set clear achievable goals. In this way you are taking charge of your life circumstances and developing the courage to move forward, beyond the hurdles you inevitably face along the way. As a student, your challenge is to counter the physical and emotional reactions to exams. As a parent or teacher, you wish to find solutions to the nagging frustration of not knowing exactly how to support your child or students.

Fran Burke is a very successful woman. She discovered early in life that if you do not take charge of your life, no one else will. Over the last twenty-six years, she has added to her coaching arsenal the likes of Life Skills Coaching, Brain Gym®, Polarity Therapy and Emotional Freedom Techniques. These are in addition to her skills as a teacher and counselor with a Master's Degree in Education on anti-bullying. Her combined skill and knowledge in these areas has given her a unique understanding of exam anxiety and how you can take charge and end it once and for all.

According to Fran, exam anxiety is really nothing to be ashamed of. With her background, Fran is well positioned to explain that, under most circumstances, exam anxiety is a natural response to a stressful situation, whereby you experience a survival or fight-flight-freeze response because you feel like your safety is being threatened. You can take a big sigh knowing that this response is normal and nothing of which to be ashamed. As well, you can take another big sigh knowing there are solutions that you can implement with powerful results.

Fran brings her brilliant solutions to the table with short-term and long-term strategies. Her short-term strategies are powerful and include the practice of Brain Gym® and Emotional Freedom Techniques. These you can start using immediately. Her long-term strategies are those you develop over time through persistence and consistency. These include the mental habit of a growth mindset, study, learning and test-taking skills, and personal self-care habits – all to support your success.

In the last year, Fran has been an active and engaged participant in my Monthly Mentor® Program. Over this time, she has intrigued other participants with her strategies for ending exam anxiety. These participants have been engaged in implementing her strategies with positive results. I was so impressed with her knowledge and skills that I encouraged her to put her approach into book form using my 10-10-10 Program™.

If you are stymied by exam anxiety, one of Fran's strategies will help you – even if you have tried things before and been no farther ahead. Most impressive is her approach of showing you

Fran Burke, M.Ed.

voluntary physical and mental actions to counter the involuntary physical and mental reaction of fight-flight-freeze. Her system is unique in the arena of exam anxiety solutions. As well, Fran suggests long-term strategies backed by the most recent discoveries in brain development and recognized by the likes of my friends Jack Canfield and Bob Proctor.

Here is a step-by-step guide to show you the way. As with anything, to gain success you need to apply the practices within this book to your own daily routines. It takes perseverance, courage and belief that you can get through this and meet exams, not with dread but with excitement instead. I wish you all the best in your transformation.

Raymond Aaron
New York Times Bestselling Author

PREFACE

When I talk about exam anxiety, I use it to include test anxiety, also. From the reading I have done and the discussions I have had, exam anxiety still flies under the radar for the majority of students, their caregivers and teachers. Now, as no time before, there are effective strategies that can be effectively practiced with amazing results. Since it appears that exam anxiety does not distinguish itself with any one particular group, and since it can afflict students with different degrees of intensity and frequency, this book is for students of all abilities and ages, their caregivers and teachers. As well, because exam anxiety is experienced by most students, I see it as a normal human response to a stressful situation rather than a pathology. This is meant to be a preventive self-help guide.

Within these pages, the "you" I am speaking to can be a senior high school, college or university student. If you are a parent or teacher looking for strategies to help the younger children/students in your care overcome exam anxiety, this book is for you, too. You will just need to change the perspective of "you" as student, to that of caregiver. Both the short-term and long-term strategies discussed in the following pages can be used with students at any age, with some adjustments needing to be made to suit the student's age and maturity.

However, please be aware that there are times when you need the help of a professional and this book is simply not enough. That time is when your anxiety is affecting other parts of your life and the techniques discussed in this book do not work to create the confidence you are striving to achieve when you face exams and other stresses in your life. A psychologist or other mental health professional can help you work through feelings, thoughts and behaviors that cause or worsen the anxiety. Ask if your school has counseling services.

I have planned out this book so that, yes, you can find out the basics of what exam anxiety is. By doing so, you will be able to recognize whether you experience it or not. Also, I show how exam anxiety has both a mental and physical component. You will learn both short-term and long-term strategies to help you reduce or eliminate exam anxiety.

I have included the short-term strategies so that you can manage your anxiety as it arises in anticipation of an exam, whether it is a day, a week or a month in advance. Of course, these strategies are also meant to be used on the day of and/or during an exam to bring calm to your mind so that you are able to take the exam with confidence. You can also use these strategies for the stress you experience after the exam, too. You will learn that some of the best short-term strategies (two of which are discussed in the following pages) for reducing the mental and physical aspects of exam anxiety also have mental and physical components to them, and this is what makes them effective. Hopefully, these will become less necessary as you develop and work from a "growth mindset" and use the other long-term strategies discussed in Unit Three of this book.

The long-term strategies I have included are equally as important to reducing exam anxiety. The first one discussed is that of the "growth mindset" identified by Dr. Carol Dweck[1]. Amongst other things it is a way to identify a key belief that you have about yourself as a learner and which affects your thoughts and behaviors as they relate to how you learn and, as part of that, how you approach exams. This mindset is fundamental to how you approach the other long-term strategies included in the pages that follow. These particular strategies include goal setting, study skills, learning methods and self-care. In all, the better you get at incorporating them into your life the more they can support your success. As you practice them, as you become more aware of how to develop a mindset that is working in your favor, these skills become easier and will support your overall success. Be sure to take them one step at a time to prevent overwhelm.

Fran Burke, M.Ed.

I have also included information about brain function and how it factors into the discussion of exam anxiety. With the advancement of neuroscience in the understanding of how the brain works, there is much more information available about what happens in the brain when you are under stress. You will learn that stress causes an involuntary reaction in the brain-body system; that is, a reaction that happens outside your control. It is called the survival response. This same involuntary reaction or reflex happens when you experience exam anxiety. As it states, this reflex action is ***involuntary*** and ***outside your initial control***. So, the question is, how can you counter this involuntary reflex? You do so by using voluntary ***action or actions*** and ***thought or thoughts*** to help bring you out of survival mode into a state in which you feel calm and in charge again. The strategies in this book help you to do just that.

Until recently, learning has been considered something that happens only in the head, and therefore emotions and the body have never really been considered important to the process of learning. This being the case, discussion with students about how natural it is for people to feel anxious at exam time can easily be overlooked by teachers and parents. Yet, its impact on your ability to do well can be enormous. In this current day and age, with a greater understanding of the power of thought and intention and with the advent of Brain Gym® and Energy Psychology, there is a greater understanding of how our thoughts impact our physiology and how techniques can be used to calm the body and bring it out of this survival reflex.

As well, talk about neuroscience and the body-brain connection and how much the integration of the two positively influences learning is new, and certainly not something that has yet been included in most teachers' trainings. One has only to consider Brain Gym®, the creation of Paul and Gail Dennison, to appreciate the important role movement with intention can play in the learning process. Or the work of Dr. Carla Hannaford, neuroscientist, educator and author of *The Dominance Factor: How Knowing Your Dominant Eye, Ear, Brain, Hand & Foot Can Improve Your Learning*[2] in which she offers a new insight into the linkages between the side of the body we favor for seeing, hearing, touching and moving and the way we think, learn, work, play and relate to others. Her work gives you a deep appreciation for the role the body plays in how well or poorly you learn in the traditional classroom. Lastly, an understanding of Energy Psychology and Emotional Freedom Techniques will help you to appreciate the profound affect your thoughts can have on you both mentally and physically.

With the advent of Brain Gym® and Energy Psychology, there are self-help strategies to address exam anxiety like never before. These systems can be used to counter involuntary reaction (fight/flight/freeze) with voluntary action and thought to bring about positive change. The strategies being offered in this book come from both of these two programs and provide these voluntary actions and thoughts to achieve the calm and confident state so desired at exam time.

So, what if you are one of a majority of students who experiences some degree of exam anxiety that does not serve you well? What if your experience is a lot more common than you think? What if this anxiety exists, but not at the level to make it a diagnosable condition? To me, what matters is that while some students are identified and get special support during exams, the majority of students do not. It is taken for granted that you will do okay. Yet, in my opinion, there are reasons to be concerned: 1.) If you do experience a heightened degree of exam anxiety and are not identified as requiring supports, then you will more than likely perform less than optimally on the exam. If this happens often enough, your future prospects can be threatened. 2.) If you experience exam anxiety often enough and do not have the tools with which to deal with it, anxiety can become neurologically hardwired into your system as a patterned response or habit when faced with a challenge of any kind. This can potentially impact your self-esteem and physical health into the future. How wonderful to have tools at an early age with which to manage anxiety and stress when it arises. It is certainly better than experiencing the mental and physical impact that ignoring or suppressing it can have on you. 3.) If you experience exam anxiety and your parents know it but do not have the tools with which to counter it, then your parents can be affected, perhaps worrying about you and feeling helpless. 4.) If teachers and schools are judged according to the success of their students and exam anxiety impacts that success, then looking at exam anxiety may be something to consider more seriously. 5.) If you experience exam anxiety, what can teachers do to mitigate against this and support you at exam time so that you can truly shine?

While the discussion in this book is about exam stress, you need to recognize that other factors taking place in your life can be affecting you, too. You may be dealing with family issues, social pressures, health issues, global concerns and/or financial matters. It is important to be aware of how these aspects of your life are supporting or not supporting your academic success and to seek out the help you need.

Here is an opportunity for you to learn about the negative impact stress might have on you at exam time and also an understanding of what happens to you physiologically and psychologically. Most importantly, how fabulous it is for you to have powerful strategies you can use to give the control back to you, the student. Is this not a gift for a lifetime?

FOR THE STUDENT

I want to congratulate you for picking up this book as I assume it is because you recognize that you experience anxiety around exams. Not everyone recognizes this or is perhaps ready to acknowledge it. And good for you for confronting it by seeking out solutions that match your needs.

I hope that you will consider your issue with exam anxiety as an opportunity to learn about yourself, to grow and develop. By facing challenges positively and discovering effective ways of meeting them, you develop and grow and become all the better for it. You empower yourself for future challenges.

Also, know that many students experience exam anxiety with different degrees of intensity.

If you are a student who experiences anxiety with almost every exam or you are a student who experiences anxiety only on certain types of exams, this book is for you. If you are a student for whom exam anxiety is a rarity but would like to know some strategies to be on the safe side, this book is also for you.

Fran Burke, M.Ed.

In this book, you will find short-term activities that you can use for in-the-moment exam anxiety relief. If at this moment you need quick relief from anxiety because you are about to face an exam in the next day or two, you have the strategies here that can help you. If you wish, you can learn them right now. It will take some time to read through each activity and to practice it. But the results can be amazingly quick. And, of course, the more you can familiarize yourself with the way to do these activities accurately, and *practice them on a regular basis*, the better will be the results.

Again, I recommend that you practice all of these activities on a consistent basis. By doing so, not only will you reduce your daily stresses but also you will be able to call on these activities immediately when the need arises before, during and even after exams. And by the way, might I suggest you also use them in preparation for and just before giving a presentation or a performance.

Next, you will find chapters that introduce you to long-term strategies for exam anxiety reduction. One chapter has to do the "growth mindset" identified by Dr. Carol Dweck. This is all about identifying the belief you have about yourself as a student and about your learning potential, and adjusting that belief if it is not serving you well. Other chapters include goal setting, study skills, learning methods and self- care. All are meant to support your success in school. By practicing and using these thought-based strategies and activities on a daily basis and backing them up with the short-term strategies for overcoming exam anxiety, you may notice a huge difference in the way you approach exams in the future. Please keep in mind that "growth mindset," study skills and self-care, when developed and practiced regularly, do get better over time. The more you incorporate them into your daily routine, the more neuropathways are developed and the better you get at them. As Malcolm Gladwell shared in his book ***Outliers***[3], it takes 10,000 hours to perfect a skill or talent.

To avoid becoming overwhelmed with these long-term strategies, you may want to read through all of them and cross out those that you use, choose one or two that you think will help you most right now and start to practice them. Once they become a routine, pick another one or two to incorporate into your daily practice.

Please be aware that there are times when you need the help of a professional and this book is simply not enough. That time is when the anxiety is affecting other parts of your life and the techniques discussed in this book do not work to accomplish the calm and confidence you are striving to achieve when you face exams and other challenges. A psychologist or other mental health professional can help you work through feelings,

Fran Burke, M.Ed.

thoughts and behaviors that cause or worsen the anxiety. Ask for the counseling services your school has to offer.

While the discussion in this book is about exam stress, you will want to recognize that other factors taking place in your life can be affecting you, too. You may be dealing with the likes of family issues, social pressures, health issues, global concerns or financial matters. It is important to be aware of how these aspects of your life are supporting or not supporting your academic success and seek out the help you need. Most importantly, be gentle with yourself.

I want to wish you well in your exam success and am confident that the information that follows will assist you to that end. May you experience calm confidence at exam time and may you shine.

FOR PARENTS/ CAREGIVERS

Are you aware if your son or daughter experiences exam anxiety? It does not matter the age. Would you know how to identify the signs that they are feeling anxious when it comes time for exams? Would you know how to help them become calmer and more confident? Do you put a lot of pressure on your child to do well on exams? Does this pressure create greater anxiety for your child?

Before you continue, I would like you to know that within the following chapters, the "you" I am speaking to can be a senior high school, college or university student. As a parent looking for strategies to help the younger children in your care overcome exam anxiety, this book is for you, too. You will need to change the perspective of "you" as student, to the perspective of caregiver. Both the short-term and long-term strategies discussed in the following pages can be used with students at any age with some adjustments needing to be made to suit the child's age and maturity.

This book is meant to be a self-help guide to support your children through their anxious moments at exam time. You will

Fran Burke, M.Ed.

be able to identify the signs of exam anxiety and share these indicators with your children, teaching them activities to help them reduce the anxious feelings and helping them develop confidence. Finally, you will be able to encourage a growth mindset, use goal setting, study skills, learning methods and self-care practices that will benefit them as they are practiced over time.

I recommend that you practice all of these activities with your children on a consistent basis. By doing so, not only will you help them reduce their daily stresses and be more prepared to learn, but you will be able to call on these activities immediately when the need arises to help them at exam time. And by the way, might I suggest you also use them with your children in preparation for and just before giving a presentation or a performance.

If you need strategies to help your child counter exam anxiety in this moment, please turn to Unit 2, Chapter 5 on Brain Gym® and Chapter 6 on Emotional Freedom Techniques. You can learn them right now. It will take some time to read through each activity and practice it. But the results can be amazingly quick. And of course the more you can familiarize yourself with the way to do these activities accurately, the better the results.

Some of the suggestions to help your children develop resilience comes from the work of Dr. Carol Dweck on what she calls a "growth mindset." Through her own research with hundreds of students, she has identified ways parents can best support their children's success. She suggests that parents support their children by helping them increase their knowledge and ways of thinking and investigating the world. As well, she suggests that parents encourage their children to regard grades as a means of understanding how well they know their subjects and what they need to do, if anything to improve their knowledge or skill in order to get better at it. In other words, in order to encourage this "growth mindset," Dweck emphasizes how important it is for parents to stress with their children that the grades they earn are the result of the effort and persistence they put into learning, and not an indication of how smart or intelligent they are. It is important to focus on the effort they made to achieve what they achieved. Furthermore, she suggests that the focus is best placed on your children meeting challenges with a positive attitude (Brain Gym® and Emotional Freedom Techniques can assist during times of struggle) and a joy of learning. She suggests this so strongly that, if parents see their children doing something that is too easy for them, they are urged to up the challenge. She suggests that parents instill in their children the value of acquiring knowledge as not only a way to contribute positively to society through the career path they choose to take in their adult lives, but to also value knowledge for its own sake. She

Fran Burke, M.Ed.

suggests that parents give their children something to strive for over time and to encourage their children to see their growth and development as a process that came about through effort and persistence. Keep your standards high for your children, she says. Praise them more for effort and persistence rather than the end achievement alone.

While the discussion in this book is about exam stress, you need to remember that other factors taking place in your children's life can be affecting them, too. They may be dealing with family issues, social pressures, health issues, global concerns or financial matters. It is important to be aware of how these aspects of their life are supporting or not supporting their academic success and seek out the help they need. Most importantly, encourage them to be gentle with themselves.

I want to wish you well as you support your children in developing confidence in the face of exams so that they can do their very best.

FOR TEACHERS

As a teacher/guidance counsellor for 24 years, a student for 18+ years, and the child of educators, the discussion of exam anxiety alluded me. It was not something that I learned in teacher training either.

Before you continue, I would like you to know that within the following chapters, the "you" I am speaking to can be a senior high school, college or university student. As a teacher looking for strategies to help the younger students in your care overcome exam anxiety, this book is for you, too. You will need to change the perspective of "you" as student, to the perspective of teacher. Both the short-term and long-term strategies discussed in the following pages can be used with students at any age, with some adjustments needing to be made to suit their age and maturity.

Recently, a friend suggested that I consider working with students who experience exam anxiety. She knew that I had worked in a secondary school for twenty-four years and that the majority of that time was spent as a guidance counsellor. She also knew that I not only had a Master's in Education degree, but had also become certified in the areas of Life Skills Coaching, Brain Gym®, Polarity Therapy and, lastly, Emotional Freedom Techniques. She felt that this was the perfect background to help students who experienced stress and worry about exams.

In fact, she wondered if I would work with an acquaintance of hers who was about to start into a pre- apprenticeship course in college. As my friend explained, this young woman had been out of school for some time and was excited to be getting into a pre-apprenticeship program with the hopes of a steady and well-paid career. It turned out that this young woman had had exam anxiety all through high school and this anxiety bothered her so much that it had already started to surface in anticipation of her being accepted into this college course. I did work with this lovely young woman and after she started to practice some of the techniques which I will share with you later in this book, she managed very well during her exams and was highly successful in completing the course.

Now, while I was more than pleased to work with this woman and go over strategies she could use to help her overcome her anxiety, I was curious about the extent to which exam anxiety was experienced amongst students. As I thought back to my own experience of writing exams, I know that there were times when I experienced anxiety and I also know that I never spoke about it, nor did anyone speak to me about it either. So here was my friend who knew something about exam anxiety that I was possibly and ashamedly unaware. I say ashamedly because as an exam writer myself and then as a teacher/counsellor, not once did I work with a student who said they experienced exam anxiety, nor was it a topic of discussion in any of my counselling department meetings. (If it were ever discussed, I expect it would have been so amongst the teachers in the department that supported students with special needs.) In fact, during exam time, any student who missed an exam was thought to be disorganized, legitimately sick, or lacked interest in doing well in school. Never, that I am aware, did one of us think that a student missed an exam because of feeling anxious! Certainly, I did not!

So here is a book that I would love to have had when I was working as a teacher and guidance counsellor. I think you will appreciate it, too. It can be a way to open discussion with your students about exam anxiety while at the same time giving you activities to practice with your students in preparation for, at the time of and after exams to help them reduce their butterflies, be calm, and shine. As well, I introduce the topic of a resilient or "growth mindset" which comes out of the research of Dr. Carol Dweck, and which I think you will find highly valuable for helping your students in many ways. Lastly, you will be able to have a discussion with your students about the study skills and personal habits that can also contribute greatly to this end result.

Dr. Dweck's basic message is that, as a teacher, it is paramount that you understand that every one of your students is developing in intelligence through effort and persistence, and that you take an interest in that development and stress with them the importance of making the effort and being persistent. These are basic keys to success. The prevalent idea that the IQ of a student is fixed is now known to be erroneous ((1) neuroscience meets this out in no uncertain terms, and (2) the test was not originally designed with the purpose to identify a fixed IQ but to determine how to help those students who were struggling to get the support they needed). So to judge each student you teach based on your idea of a fixed IQ is contrary to her "growth mindset" message. She emphasizes the importance of teachers praising their students for hard work and effort and recognizing *this* as the basis of success. She gives numerous examples of people who have risen to the top of their chosen field and who were considered to be no more than average when they were in school. She attributes their consistent and persistent effort and a love for their field of endeavor as the determining factors to their success.

While the discussion in this book is about exam stress, please remember that other factors taking place in your students' lives can be affecting them, too. They may be dealing with the likes of family issues, social pressures, health issues, global concerns or financial matters. It is important to be aware of how these aspects of their lives are supporting or not supporting their academic success and seek out the help they need. Most importantly, encourage them to be gentle with themselves.

ABOUT THE AUTHOR

I worked as an educator—four years as a teacher and 20 years as a guidance counsellor at the high school level. As part of my continuing education I specialized in anti-bullying in my Masters in Education degree and became certified in four practices—Life Skills, Brain Gym®, Polarity Therapy and Emotional Freedom Techniques. These modalities offer, amongst many other things, very effective self-help strategies to overcome challenges in life, like exam anxiety.

My parents were both educators. In all my years as a child of educators, as a student (18+ years in total) and as a teacher and counsellor (24 years in total), the topic of exam anxiety was rarely discussed.

Despite the fact that my father was a university professor and my mother later became an elementary school French teacher, the topic of exam anxiety never surfaced as a topic of conversation at the dinner table. It is understandable that my parents would carry on in their adult life what they experienced when they were growing up. I expect that when they were in school no one ever recognized or talked much about this thing called exam anxiety, either. And if someone did experience it, maybe they felt awkward talking about it. Maybe back then students were told just deal with it, that is, if it were mentioned at all. In any case, maybe like me, they did experience exam anxiety in one form or another. Were they aware of what was happening? Perhaps. Did they have ways to prevent it? Perhaps, but more than likely not.

My parents were very busy. My father was a full-time professor at university, and my mother cared for the children, eight in all. Then, once the youngest was independent enough, my mother took up teaching. There was not much time or awareness of the need to devote to feelings, and I was not accustomed to baring my soul to either of my parents as they were not accustomed to sharing their feelings either. In fact, my family did not deal well with emotion at all. It was not until after I graduated from university that I started to develop a language for emotion and started to make connections between the thoughts I had and how I felt emotionally and physically. So, it is not a stretch to say that I was unaware of the impact that exams had on me, except to say, that I now know that I was in survival mode most of the time. It never occurred to me to tell anyone how I felt at the time I was writing exams. While I did not experience debilitating exam anxiety for every exam – I experienced it at different times, with varying intensity and for different reasons, as you will read below.

How to End Exam Anxiety

I remember cheating on an exam in grade five—that was my survival tactic at the time. My family had just moved across the continent of the United States to a town in Minnesota, one of many moves we made over the years. Everyone in my family was adjusting to our new home as my mother and father were getting it set up to accommodate all of their seven children and the eighth baby on the way. Besides, I was in grade five and finding it no easy matter to fit in and make friends in an all-too-cliquey class of grade fivers. Not only were the cliques already well-established and closed to outsiders, but one's popularity and acceptance depended partly on how well one could play baseball. For me, this was a big deal because where I had come from, girls did not play baseball. As you can imagine, I was not a first pick when teams were being chosen! My efforts during my grade-five year were greatly focused on making friends.

So you might ask, what does all that have to do with exam anxiety? Well, directly perhaps, nothing.

However, indirectly, it has a lot to do with it. You see, I was so distracted by this need to fit in and adjust to a new town that I am sure my attention was more absent than present when I was in the classroom. So was I learning what the teacher was teaching? Did I hear the teacher announce that we would be having an exam? Was I able to study at home? Probably not. So, sometimes the stress of writing an exam is caused by external factors like mine.

I remember sitting in the last row at the back of the class. Perhaps there were five or six aisles across and only two of us sat in the last row across an aisle from each other. The teacher gave the instruction to clear our desk by putting all our books under our chairs, and to keep only a pencil with an eraser with which to write the test. Then, the student sitting in front of me passed me the exam. As was the practice, I printed my name in the top right-hand corner and waited for the teacher to tell us to start. As I read through the exam, I could answer only a few of the numerous questions. When I found it safe, I motioned to the student across the aisle from me to tell me the answers. This she did and for this I was grateful. Feeling very stressed, I finished the exam and handed it in.

Now, to this day, I do not remember what we were tested on. I do still feel badly that I cheated; I do wonder what impression I left on the student who helped me. And, to this day, I wonder if I was really all that good at cheating. What I prefer to think is that my teacher saw me cheating, said nothing simply because she had compassion for me, knowing all that I was going through adjusting to a new life in a new town with all its challenges.

Now, what I also know is that I was in survival mode and in this case fighting for best results.

Fast forward a few years, to my senior year in high school, and the time for me had come to take my Scholastic Aptitude Tests (SATs). In retrospect, my parents were not at all supportive of my efforts to study and write these formidable exams. Surprising, considering their educational backgrounds. Nevertheless, I got the study manuals and studied on my own. The motivation to study and take these exams came more because all the other students were doing so and not because I had chosen a program to study at a specific college or university or knew what scores I needed in order to achieve this goal. (How sad that I never heard about goal setting until I had graduated from university and was going through training as a Life Skills Coach.) And of course, there was an inordinate amount of stress my friends had connected to taking the SATs—getting good scores determined where they went to college. And as you might imagine, the night before the exams, I did what everyone else did; I stayed up all night studying. When, just before the exam, I was offered a little white pill to stay awake; like everyone else in my group, I took it. To this day, I do not know what the pill was or how I did on the exams. Not knowing the results of the exam might seem strange; however, I attribute it in part to the fact that my parents really took no interest in what I had done, and to the fact that my scores were probably not that stellar.

Fran Burke, M.Ed.

Only later in the school year did I understand why my parents had taken no interest. All along, they had been planning to move to Canada and knew that any results I achieved on my SATs would not matter for entrance into a Canadian university anyway.

What does this have to do with exam anxiety? I must admit, I was going through the motions, not really connected to the results in the same way I imagine the other students were. One practice that is, of course, strongly advised against is pulling an all-nighter—that is, staying up the entire night before the exam studying, and then believing one can achieve excellent results on the exam the next day. This practice is often the result of poor study habits, a "fixed mindset," and an anxiety that one has not learned everything that is needed for success. As you can imagine, not only was I exhausted for the SAT, but the "little white pill" made me feel ill. Thankfully for me, it was of no real consequence.

I was in survival mode, operating from an act/react way of being.

Fast forward to my sophomore-year in university. I was faced with writing my final exam in Art History and not at all confident that I could do well. So my survival response kicked in. I feigned being sick.

How to End Exam Anxiety

In this case, my survival mode was to flee. Luckily for me, the professor accepted my doctor's note and excused me from the exam altogether. My final mark for the course was not compromised—an anomaly I believe. Most students would have been penalized for missing a final exam.

Does any of this sound familiar to you? Although at the time I did not realize it, I simply found ways to survive. And like most other people, when I am in survival, my ways of managing what is demanded of me are not always ideal. How about you? I was not aware of what I was doing at the time. I was simply surviving the demands being made of me over the span of years I was in school.

Now, during my adult years as a teacher and guidance counsellor in high school, I must confess that once again the topic of exam anxiety was seldom, if ever, discussed. Sure, I helped students in many positive and supportive ways. The main focus I had in my guidance career was helping students transition successfully to high school and then again to work, college or university. It is well known that the transition to high school can create much anxiety for students and even cause some to drop out. While I did much to help make the transition for them into high school as seamless as possible, all the while supporting them so that they would be confident on their first day and throughout their first year, I now realize that I never

Fran Burke, M.Ed.

once mentioned the word anxiety or any of its manifestations. In fact, I created a PowerPoint for the incoming students with the title, "Surviving Your 10th Grade Year." In retrospect, I would now replace the word "surviving" with "thriving" and share with them the significant difference between these two ways of being. Once the students were settled in their first year and onwards, my focus was mostly helping them choose their courses according to their post-secondary plans. Above all, I wanted to know that all of my students had the requirements to achieve their post-secondary goal and were working confidently toward it.

Surprisingly, throughout all these years, not once did students confide in me that they needed help dealing with exam anxiety. When it came time for final exams at the end of each semester, there were ever-so-many students who would miss their exams. Occasionally, students would follow up an absence with a doctor's note, but never once did we consider the possibility that a student's absence was due to anxiety. Rather it was attributed to a student's lack of organization, time management, not writing down the time of the exam correctly, and an "I couldn't care less" attitude.

Now, one might say, "If no one talks about exam anxiety, maybe it doesn't exist after all." To the contrary. Not only do I have my own experience with exam anxiety, but over the past months, I have been talking to people about how I now support students who experience exam anxiety. When they hear what I am doing, I am amazed and frankly shocked at what people have told me. I have found that it is far more common than I had ever imagined. I have heard of students quitting school because they could not handle the stress of exams; students sent to emergency because they started hyperventilating; students freezing and not being able to think well enough to retrieve the information for which they had studied so well; students having stomach issues; most recently a student who throws up; students who sweat profusely and experience a rapid heartbeat; and the list goes on. In most of these situations, the individuals did know they were experiencing exam anxiety but did not have a means to do anything to stop it. Not only did the students not have the tools with which to reduce the anxiety, the parents were at a loss to help, also. What about their teachers? How aware were they of how their students were feeling?

I came from a family situation where the children were not pressured into getting high marks, although this pressure is very real for many students. I did come from a family culture where my parents wanted their children to choose their own career path. In fact, I do not remember ever having a discussion about my future career with my parents at all. I was one who wanted

Fran Burke, M.Ed.

to be a nurse but did not ever find out what courses I needed to take, what marks I needed to earn or what college or university to attend for this purpose.

How well I did or did not do in school was not just about managing exam anxiety. Much had to do with my family life. I was fortunate that my parents made sure my siblings and I were home on weeknights getting our homework done and getting to bed at a decent hour. I was fortunate that they had developed the discipline and skill of studying and valued it enough to help us when we were struggling. While they valued education for us all, they did not put any kind of pressure on us to get high marks. Perhaps they knew how this could create too much stress for us and how harmful this could be. They encouraged us to do the best we could do. Surprisingly, despite their educational backgrounds, they did not connect the education we were getting with possible careers in adulthood, nor did they help us have a plan. I somehow had my sights set on nursing. However, during the years I was in high school, no one ever talked to me about what I had to study or what marks I needed to earn in order to get into a nursing program, and I did not know enough to inquire. So in the only conversation I had with a "guidance counsellor" I was told that I did not have the math requirements to get into nursing. I was only told this after my high school graduation.

I have concluded that we pass on to the upcoming generation what we experience in school. My parents passed on their lack of awareness of exam anxiety to their children and their students, no doubt. I, in turn, have followed suit with the students in the school where I taught and counselled. If exam anxiety is not mentioned and the symptoms are not described, it is not possible for students to give voice to what they experience—just like me. If it is not mentioned and the signs not described, students could very possibly think that their experience is the norm and to know no difference, especially if they have not been given the language to describe it. Or, if it is not mentioned and the signs not described, students may not know to say anything about what they are experiencing—just like me. If it is not mentioned and the signs not described, perhaps students think of it as a weakness and are ashamed to mention it. And, if they do, they may just be told to relax, or too bad, or suck it up.

Just recently, I asked a young woman who graduated in the spring of 2015 from a year of teacher training if she had received any training about exam anxiety. She said that there was no mention of it. Nothing was taught about what it is, how it is experienced or how to help students achieve calm in the face of exams. Here again I repeat that we pass on from one generation to the next what we have learned and experienced. When I was in teacher training, no mention was made of exam anxiety either.

Fran Burke, M.Ed.

Various factors determine the outcome on exams: external factors such as home and social life; being aware of the self-talk that contributes to exam anxiety; knowing how to study and set goals for oneself; having the language and awareness of the difference between feeling confident or anxious; and having the strategies and awareness to overcome the stress when it arises. How valuable to have such strategies at an early age to help empower students during their school years. Needless to say, the benefits will last a lifetime.

[1] Dweck, Carol, Ph.D. *Mindset: The new Psychology of Success.* New York, Random House. 2006

[2] Hannaford, Carla, Ph.D. *The Dominance Factor; How Knowing Your Dominant Eye, Ear, Brain, Hand & Foot Can Improve Your Learning.* Salt Lake City, Great River Books. 1997.

[3] Gladwell, Malcom. *Outliers: The Story of Success.* London, England. Penguin Books. 2009.

prepared for the exam. Yet, when it was time to actually write the exam you froze; you could not remember the material of which you studied so much.

Here is an example of that situation: Recently, I had a chat with a school principal who mentioned how, in university, he had to write an accounting exam and had this very same experience. He said that he was not one to have exam anxiety, so this experience was new. When he sat down to write the exam, his mind went blank. He sat for much of the exam time just trying to remember. Finally, he relaxed enough to answer some of the questions before the time was up; he barely passed the exam. His results certainly did not reflect what he knew.

Who Experiences Exam Anxiety?

It is common for students of any age and any culture to experience exam anxiety. It can arise from a belief about oneself. If you believe that passing an exam shows that you are intelligent, and failing it indicates that you are less than intelligent, there is much to concern you. It may well arise if you have external pressures. For example, it may be especially difficult to face an exam if you feel that your standing with your parents, friends and others is determined by the results. Or, what if you are afraid that your future job prospects hang in the balance because of poor exam results? This may create a very real pressure to do well. Extreme fear can be a detriment to learning, and can lead to poor exam performance. Much depends upon the pressures that are weighing on you—and the severity of the anxiety.

On the other hand, there are some students for whom feeling a little nervous can help to make them feel alert, and prepared to handle the exam. It could be that anxiety is really due to an eagerness to show what they know, prove what they have learned, eager to face yet one more challenge.

At What Age Does Exam Anxiety Start?

I know a mother of a grade-three student. Her child experiences exam anxiety. That being the case she was very pleased that I was writing this book, and looked forward to reading it. She wants to know how to calm her son, and make him confident at exam time.

Here is a young child already experiencing exam anxiety. According to Dweck, at a very young age children are sensitive about how people evaluate them. As a result, the children themselves become sensitive and judge themselves when they excel or perform poorly. She states that every word and action of adults sends a message from which children will develop either a "growth mindset" or a "fixed mindset."

It can be a fixed mindset message that says: **You have permanent traits and I'm judging them.** *Or it can be a growth-mindset message that says:* **You are a developing person and I am interested in your development.**[3]

Children are sensitive and concerned about the messages they receive. Surprisingly, after seven experiments with hundreds of children, Dweck found very clearly that "Praising children's intelligence harms their motivation and it harms their performance."[4] She goes on to explain that children interpret the praise of being smart as equal to having no challenges or failures. Thus, when they experience something that is difficult their confidence is threatened because they believe they are not living up the intelligent or smart child they have been told they are. In turn, this causes them to lose motivation. If they have challenges or experience failure that means, in their eyes, they are dumb. If they do things well and are told how smart they are or what quick learners they are, they evaluate themselves accordingly and put this expectation on themselves for everything. As a consequence, they can become self-conscious and lose that eagerness to get better at something if it means that they may fail at it in the early learning stages. And they may equate effort and hard work with being dumb. If they are constantly praised for their intelligence, their quick learning ability, and their character, they will begin to equate their identity with that.

With that in mind, exam anxiety can begin as early as elementary school. If mom and dad, caretakers and teachers reinforce exam results in the context of how smart you are, when you are faced with an exam, *your entire self is at risk* if you are not able to maintain the score that matches that expectation. The focus moves away from what you know, how much you have learned, the joy of finding out how much you have learned, the effort you made, the importance of persistence, and what more you still need to learn to pass this exam, to whether or not you can live up to the intelligent and able person you are told you are. Success is not fixed. There is no such thing as being perfect in any particular subject, skill, behavior, etc. It is a process.

What Is the Cause of Exam Anxiety?

Exam anxiety is really caused by the beliefs you have and the thoughts you think—either at the conscious or subconscious level. This goes for students of all ages. It can start with the messages that you get from other students, teachers or parents. These thoughts lead to neurological and physiological reactions, and to unwanted behaviors. Let us look at some of these beliefs and thoughts that contribute to exam anxiety.

Some of the thoughts you have can be about your sense of self-worth. Do you feel good about yourself, despite the grades you earn, or do you equate your self-worth with the marks you receive? Is it possible that you have had poor exam results in the past or had difficulty on some exams and these negative experiences are hard for you to shake? Is it possible that you were embarrassed in some way by a poor exam result or the answer you gave in class? What about the expectation your parents, family and friends have of you? Do you feel you can live up to their expectations and fear what will happen if you do not?

Are you aware of your self-talk? Is your self-talk mostly positive or is it negative? Your self-talk is determined by your own personal nature and also from past experience. It is important to become aware of what you say to yourself and to find tools to help replace the negative self-talk to the positive (for this you can refer to the chapter on Emotional Freedom Techniques and the chapter on Self-Care).

According to the Metropolitan Community College, Kansas City *Students who have exam anxiety are prone to negative self-talk. Exam anxiety can be generated or heightened by repeatedly making statements to yourself that usually begin with "what if." For example, "What if I fail the exam?" or "What if I fail this class again?" These "what if" statements generate more anxiety which can cause students to feel sick. These statements tell them to be anxious. Some other aspects of self-talk are:*

- *Self-talk can be in telegraphic form with short words or images.*
- *Self-talk can be illogical but at the time the person believes it.*
- *Negative self-talk can lead to avoidance like not taking the exam or skipping classes.*
- *Negative self-talk can lead to depression and a feeling of helplessness.*
- *Negative self-talk is a bad habit which can be changed.*

Furthermore, the Metropolitan Community College indicates that there are different types of negative self-talk. If you use negative self-talk, then review the types below and see which one fits you best. You may use a combination of them:

A. **The Critic** is the person inside us who is always trying to put us down. It constantly judges behaviors and finds fault even if it is not there. It jumps on any mistake and exaggerates it to cause more anxiety. The Critic puts us down for mistakes on the exam and blames us for not controlling the anxiety. The Critic reminds us of previous comments from real people who have criticized us. It compares us to other students who are doing better in the class. It loves to say, "That was a stupid mistake!" or "You are a total disappointment. You can't pass this math class like everyone else can!" The Critic's goal is to promote low self-esteem.

B. **The Worrier** is the person inside us who looks at the worst-case scenario. It wants to scare us with the ideas of disasters and complete failure. When it sees the first sign to anxiety, it "blows it out of proportion" to the extent that we will not remember anything and totally fail the exam. The Worrier creates more anxiety than normal. The Worrier anticipates the worst, underestimates our ability, and sees us not only failing the exam but "failing life." The Worrier loves to ask "What if?" For example, "What if I fail the math exam and don't graduate?" or "What if I can't control my anxiety and throw up in math class?" The goal of the Worrier is to cause more anxiety so we will quit.

C. **The Victim** is the person inside us who wants us to feel helpless or hopeless. It wants us to believe that no matter what we do, we will not be successful in math. The Victim does not blame other events (poor schooling) or people (bad teachers) for math failures. It blames us. It dooms us and puts us into a learned helpless mode, meaning that if we try to learn math, we will fail, or if we don't try to learn math we will fail. So why try? The Victim likes to say, "I can't learn math." The goal of the Victim is to cause depression and make us not try.

D. **The Perfectionist** is similar to the Critic, but is the opposite of the Victim. It wants us to do the best we can and will guide us into doing better. It tells us that we are not studying enough for the math exam and that a B is not good enough and that we must make an A. In fact, sometimes an A is not good enough unless it is a 100%. So, if we make a B on the exam the Perfectionist says, "A or

B is just like making an F." The Perfectionist is the hard-driving part of us that wants the best but cannot stand mistakes or poor grades. It can drive us to mental and physical exhaustion to make that perfect grade. It is not interested in self-worth, just perfect grades. Students driven by the Perfectionist often drop a math course because they only have a B average. The Perfectionist loves to repeat, "I should have. . ." or "I must. . ." The goal of the Perfectionist is to cause chronic anxiety that leads to burnout.[5]

Self-talk takes place at a subconscious level. You need to tune in to find out what your self-talk is before you can change it. To help replace the negative to positive self-talk please refer to the chapter on Emotional Freedom Techniques and on Self-Care.

The Twelve Myths of Exam Anxiety:

- Students are born with exam anxiety.
- Exam anxiety is a mental illness.
- Exam anxiety cannot be reduced.
- Any level of exam anxiety is bad.
- All students who are not prepared have exam anxiety.
- Students with exam anxiety cannot learn math.
- Students who are well prepared will not have exam anxiety.
- Very intelligent students and students taking high-level courses, such as calculus, do not have exam anxiety.

- Attending class and doing your homework should reduce all your exam anxiety.
- Being told to relax during an exam will make you relaxed.
- Doing nothing about exam anxiety will make it go away.
- Reducing exam anxiety will guarantee better grades."[6]

[1] http://www.amaon.com/*Lexicon-Websters-Dictionary-Language-Encyclopedic*/dp/071

[2] http://www.therapists.com/fundamentals/exam-anxiety

[3] Dweck, Carol, Ph.D. *Mindset: The New Psychology of Success.* New York, Random House.2006. p. 173

[4] Dweck, Carol, Ph.D. *Mindset: The New Psychology of Success.* New York, Random House. 2006. P. 175.

[5] http://mcckc.edu/common/services/BR_Tutoring/files/math/study:skills/

[6] http://www.mcckc.edu/pdf/Counseling/manage_test_anxiety.pdf Metropolitan Community College, Kansas City

CHAPTER 2
Exam Anxiety and the Survival Response

What is the Survival Response?

What happens in your brain and body when you experience anxiety? When you experience stress or anxiety, such as you do at exam time, there is a physiological reaction that takes place in your brain and body called the survival or the fight-flight-freeze response. For our distant cousins, this survival response was essential because it kept them safe from harm, whether from a sabre-toothed tiger or from an enemy. By going into this involuntary survival response, our remote ancestors would have either had the energy to fight the enemy or the perseverance to flee to safety because the small nerve bundle called the amygdala in the brain would have immediately responded by sending a signal through the thalamus to the adrenal glands to flood the blood stream with adrenalin. With this taking place, our ancestors' digestive tract would become constricted and blood would have been forced to the hands and feet, preparing the body with the strength to fight or the perseverance to flee. Once the threat was over, these remote relatives of ours would have gone back to a relaxed state until the next threat occurred.

Unless there were constant threats to safety or our ancestors succumbed to the enemy, they would have been able to recover from the experience and return to a more relaxed, calm state.

In current times, this same response takes place when you feel stressed, overwhelmed and have difficulty coping with daily demands. And because these demands are often constant in your life, you tend to live in survival mode much of the time. Exam anxiety is one example of the kind of stressors that cause this basic human reaction.

Why the Survival Response Happens

The survival response is a life-saving response when it is triggered by life-threatening situations, real or perceived. According to Bruce Lipton, award-winning researcher and author and speaker on the New Biology, first and foremost, your physiology is hard-wired to protect you. Secondly, your physiology is hard-wired to grow and heal. Your body is either in survival mode or in growth/healing mode. It cannot be in both modes optimally at the same time.[1]

While you are not threatened by sabre-toothed tigers in this day and age, there are many triggers that cause you to live constantly in this survival state with excess adrenaline and cortisol flowing in your veins, and the blood at your extremities ready for fight-

or-flight. It is not just the pressure of writing exams. Consider the demands on your time, finances, attention, and energy, as they relate to the roles you have in your life as student, child, sibling, friend, employee, parent, etc. If these demands are too overwhelming and cause stress, the automatic response is that of survival. Adrenalin is pumped into the body and cortisol will follow.

Now, consider the anxiety you experience related to exams. The survival response kicks in to keep you safe and to protect you. It is an automatic response, a reflex and is not rational. Your body will respond in ever-so-many ways, and as a result, your thought processes may be less than optimal. In fight mode, you might decide to cheat on your exams. In freeze mode, you may not be able to think or retrieve the information you studied so hard to learn. In flight mode, you may feign being sick and avoid the exam or turn to alcohol or drugs to quell the stress. Needless to say, this survival reflex works against your best interest to do well on your exams.

What Happens in the Brain and Body during the Survival Response?

A change happens in the brain/body system. The survival response is driven by the part of the brain, called the hind brain or brain stem. In this survival state, an individual is not able to process information using the limbic (midbrain) or prefrontal cortex in the forebrain area where rational thought and executive function take place. Thus, rather than thinking rationally, one is operating from the act/react or fight-flight-freeze response of the hindbrain. When stress is chronic, nerve nets to the frontal lobes are less likely to develop and this can result in learning difficulties and a lessened ability to control your behaviors, plan and follow through on such plans. Frontal lobe functioning is essential to learning. It is here that self-control, executive function and reasoning take place.[2] And higher and more prolonged levels of cortisol circulating in the body have detrimental effects on your well-being. It is shown to affect memory, learning potential, and to impair cognitive function.[3]

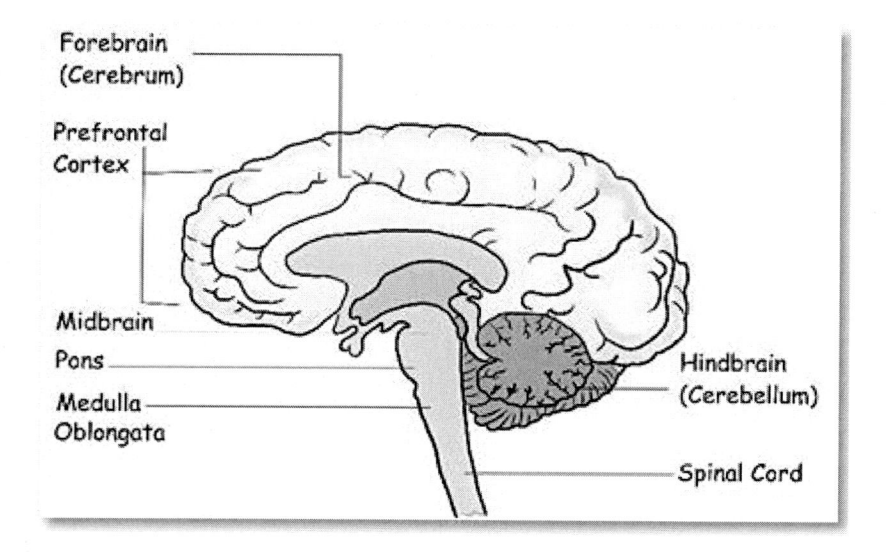

How to End Exam Anxiety

As a reflex response to the perception of danger, your body releases adrenalin from your kidneys to flood the blood stream for the strength and perseverance needed to survive. The blood flows to your hands and the feet to prepare to fight or to flee. The fact that the blood flows away from the digestive tract explains why anxiety and stress can cause problems with your digestive functions. This impacts your body's ability to digest and absorb the food that you have consumed. The cortisol created as part of this survival response is known to increase stomach fat, to cause sleep disruption, to lower bone density, and to dampen thyroid function[4]. As well, your eyes move peripherally so they can take in as much of the environment as possible. This makes it extremely difficult for your eyes to team and track across a page of writing.

A colleague of mine shared with me that her exam and presentation anxiety took the form of diarrhea. It was a running joke (no pun intended) in her family. They knew every time she had to write an exam or give a presentation because she spent an inordinate amount of time in the bathroom. How unfortunate that she had to suffer this way and that her reaction was considered no more than a "joke" on the part of her parents who no doubt and sadly had no way of helping her.

In his book ***The Biology of Belief,*** Bruce Lipton states that there are two behaviors that are fundamental for any living creature to survive. One is growth/repair and the other is protection. He goes on to say that the two cannot exist optimally at the same time. When energy is used for protection/survival, energy for growth and repair is lacking. Thus, for health reasons, the more we can manage to be in the state of calm, the more we can maintain our health.

As noted above, exam anxiety stimulates the survival response in the body. This survival response is often triggered by how we perceive what is taking place in our lives as a threat.

According to Dr. Carla Hannaford, other causes can contribute to a survival response, too. In her book, *SMART MOVES Why Learning Is Not All in Your Head*, Hannaford identifies some of these stress- inducing triggers that keep students today in constant survival mode and make it difficult for them to access their prefrontal cortex where higher order thinking takes place. Some of these include:

- ***Developmental*** *—lack of sensory stimulation, lack of movement, lack of touch, lack of interactive creative play and communication, unbalanced or incomplete RAS activation*
- ***Electrical*** *—inadequate water consumption, inadequate oxygen, excessive exposure to external EMFs*

- **Nutritional**—inadequate amounts of proteins, lack of essential amino acids and fatty acids, high carbohydrate and sugar diets
- **Medical**—low birth weight babies, chronic middle ear infections, allergies, medications, yeast overgrowth, inadequate diet or sleep, substance abuse, child abuse, poor vision or hearing.
- **TV, computers and video games**—which can lead to violence, decreased imaginative development, less interactive communication, ocular lock, decreased motor development, decreased motivation, and linear thinking that lacks comprehension of complex systems.
- **Competition**— inappropriate expectations (at home, school, work or self-imposed), pressures towards social conformity, competition in sports and in the arts, learning in a winner/loser rather than cooperative framework. Rigid educational systems— developmentally inappropriate curricula, constant low-level skills testing, lecture/writing formats for quiet classrooms, unawareness of or inattention to unique learning style.[5]

Powerful Ways to Counter the Survival Response

To appreciate how Brain Gym® and Emotional Freedom Techniques can help you counter the anxiety you experience at exam time (the period during which you are studying for an exam and at the time of an exam), it will help to understand not only what happens in your body/brain system when it is under such stress, but also why it happens. While exam anxiety is experienced at specific times, other stress factors in life (should they exist at exam time, and they often do) can exacerbate this anxiety, too.

All of the indicators of exam anxiety that are listed below are the result of what is called the stress response or the flight-flight-freeze response discussed above. Because you do not run or fight to use up the adrenalin and other chemicals produced during this time of survival, other reactions take place in the body instead. These are the "symptoms" of anxiety. I like to call them indicators in order to avoid pathologizing them.

When used, both Brain Gym® and Emotional Freedom Techniques have the power to counter the survival response that accompanies stress and anxiety. By using them, you may regain confidence and control for clearer thinking, learning and studying. These will be discussed in Unit 2.

[1] Church, Dawson and Allenby, Sasha. *Matrix Reimprinting Using EFT; Rewrite Your Past, Transform Your Future*. United Kingdom, Hay House. 2010. P.34.

[2] Hannaford, Carla, Ph.D. *Smart Moves; Why Learning Is Not All In Your Head*. Salt Lake City, Great River Books, 2005. Pp. 144-145

[3] Church, Dawson and Allenby, Sasha. *Matrix Reimprinting Using EFT; Rewrite Your Past, Transform Your Future.* United Kingdom, Hay House. 2010. P. 36.

[4] Lipton, Bruce. *The Biology of Belief.* Hay House Publishing. USA. 2008. Pp 115-116.

[5] Hannaford, Carla, Ph.D. *Smart Moves, Why Learning Is Not All In Your Head.* Salt Lake City. Great River Books. 2005. P. 147.

CHAPTER 3
Indicators of Exam Anxiety

As mentioned earlier, all of the indicators of exam anxiety that are listed below are the result of what is called the Stress Response or the Flight-Flight-Freeze response. Because you do not run or fight to use up the adrenaline and other chemicals released for survival, alternative reactions take place in the body. These are the "symptoms" of anxiety. I like to call them indicators.

There are many possible reactions that may result from this survival-response you experience with exam anxiety. As you will learn later, thoughts can flow from the conscious or subconscious mind. These thoughts may be negative. The exam anxiety indicators listed below are from The Anxiety and Depression Association of America[1], and www.therapists.com/fundamentals/exam-anxiety[2].

I recommend that you be proactive on exam days. What do I mean by that? First, I suggest that you reflect on past experiences when you faced an exam. Reflect on what you have experienced in the past; on how you had prepared. How confident or not was your thinking? How did you feel as you looked at the sheet of questions? Consider how aware you were of your experience. Was there a good feeling? What was the feeling? Did you ever discuss exam anxiety with anyone . . . or did you stuff it down, hoping that you would be okay? What did you do to help yourself with the problem?

Now, as you read through the list of indicators below, see which ones apply to you. This information may give you insights about yourself, your thoughts, and how you respond to exam anxiety. The greater your awareness, the better. The first step is awareness, the second step is wanting solutions, and the third step is finding solutions that work for you. The last step is using the solutions you have found. Keep reading.

1. Behavioral Indicators

Your beliefs and attitudes lead to your behaviors. What mindset could prompt you to forsake exam preparation (with the exception of those students who need to work to earn money while they are studying) until the last minute, and then cause you to stay up all night cramming before an exam? What causes you to be lackluster in your studies? What is it that prevents you from developing good study habits? Do you skip classes regularly? Why?

What beliefs and attitudes do you have about studying and about exams? Some examples might be:

- I don't have time to study and it doesn't do me any good anyway.
- I hate to study. I'd prefer to _____
- What's the point? There are no jobs after I graduate anyway.
- It's not cool to study.
- I have better things to do. What better things? Explain.
- Only stupid kids should have to study. If I study, that means I'm stupid. (Einstein studied every day of his life.)

Now you can list your beliefs and attitudes. Which ones help you to study and develop the confidence you need to do well on exams?

-
-

-
-
-
-

Other behavioral indicators can be:

a. Difficulty concentrating
b. Fidgeting
c. Pacing
d. Substance abuse
e. Avoidance of the exam
f. Dropping out of school
g. Procrastination
h. Last-minute cramming

People find a way to succeed. They know that effort is required, they know what motivates them and they know they must persist—until they get it. There is no Royal Road to success.

2. Organizational Indicators

Poor organization can certainly lead to exam anxiety. Good management of your time, space, materials, etc. produces big dividends. Personal habits e.g. getting enough rest, having a nutritious diet, rising at a reasonable hour, depending on your list of tasks for the day.

Poor organization can result from anxiety. If anxiety is such that it prevents you from being able to focus and attend to detail, organization will suffer.

Organization can include everything from having a backpack and an agenda book. It can mean color coding your materials by class, and having a morning routine. It can mean knowing when assigned projects are due. It means taking action, and setting aside time every day towards the completion of tasks.

Please go to the Study Skills section of Unit 3 of this book to find out more about organization.

3. Physical Indicators

As mentioned above, one of the physiological reactions that arises when you experience exam anxiety is that the body goes into survival mode. According to Bruce Lipton, award-winning researcher, author and speaker on New Biology, when you go into survival mode, your body cannot be healing or building at the same time.[3] This is because the sympathetic nervous system, designed to keep us safe, takes precedence over the para-sympathetic nervous system designed for growth and healing. What happens when we become anxious is that blood fills with adrenalin and leaves the core of the body away from the digestive tract and vital organs to go to the hands and the feet. This is where the adrenalin-rich blood and oxygen is needed in order to fight or to flee.

It is not surprising that many of the indicators of exam anxiety are experienced in the stomach because there is not enough blood to help with digestion and elimination. Notice these and the others that affect other parts of the body, too.

a. Rapid heartbeat
b. Vomiting
c. Diarrhea
d. Unable to focus your eyes
e. Dry mouth
f. Headache
g. Nausea
h. Excessive sweating
i. Light-headedness
j. Tension
k. Feeling faint
l. "Butterflies" in the stomach
m. Shaking of the hands and feet
n. Extreme body temperature
o. Shortness of breath

4. Mental indicators

a. Freeze response and unable to remember what you studied
b. Difficulty understanding questions
c. Difficulty organizing your thoughts

d. Comparing self to others
e. Difficulty concentrating
f. Going blank
g. Difficulty remembering
h. Self-doubt

5. Emotional indicators
a. Anger
b. Fear
c. Helplessness
d. Depression
e. Excessive crying or laughing
f. Disappointment

6. Dominance Factor[4]

One physiological factor that has just recently been identified in the field of neuroscience. It is called the Dominance Factor. This factor, which Dr. Carla Hannaford, neuroscientist, outlines in her book, *The Dominance Factor: How Knowing Your Dominant Eye, Ear, Brain, Hand & Foot Can Improve Your Learning*, shows the link between the side of the body you favor for seeing, hearing, touching and moving and the way you think, learn, work, play and relate to others.

Hannaford has been able to demonstrate that you have developed a unique way of doing things, neurologically. Consider that the left brain hemisphere connects to the right side of the body and controls the right eye, ear, hand and foot. The right brain hemisphere connects to the left side of the body and controls the left eye, ear, hand and foot. When you are able to access both brain hemispheres equally, you are in a fully integrated state. It is in this state that learning and performing are easiest.

Now consider that, like everyone, you were born with your preferred brain hemisphere, as well as your preferred eye, ear, hand and foot. Another way to say it is that one brain hemisphere is more dominant than the other, and the same goes for having a dominant eye, ear, hand and foot. Either you were born right brain dominant or left brain dominant. You were born either right or left eye dominant, right or left ear dominant, right or left hand dominant, and right or left foot dominant.

So how does this relate to exam anxiety? Remember: learning and performing are easiest when you are able to access both brain hemispheres equally, because you are in a fully integrated state. For example, you are able to take in the whole picture (right brain function) and get the detail (left brain function), too. When you are anxious, you lose this integrated state and default to your preferred dominance; the non-preferred hemisphere, eye, ear, hand and foot are not as accessible to you.

If your left brain hemisphere is dominant, and so are your right eye, ear, hand and foot dominant, then you have access to one side of the body and can function fairly well under stress. The reverse is also true. If you are right brain hemisphere dominant and left eye, ear, hand and foot dominant, then you have access to one side of the body and can function fairly well under stress. However, because you are not in a fully integrated state, you are not able to learn and express yourself fully.

Interestingly, you may find that you have a mixed dominance profile. As an example, you may be left brain dominant and rather than having a dominant right eye, ear, and hand and foot, you could have a dominant right eye, dominant left ear, dominant left hand, and a dominant right foot. Under stress, you would default to your left hemisphere, right eye and right foot and lose easy access to your left ear and left hand.

Consider that the left brain hemisphere is typically the logic hemisphere. It processes in such a way that it starts with the pieces first, processes the parts of language, the syntax, the semantics, the letters, sentences, and numbers. It is the side of the brain that analyzes, looks for differences, controls feelings, is planned and structured, sequential in thinking, is future-oriented, is about technique and sports (hand-eye/foot placement), in art (media, tool use, how to) and music (notes, beat, tempo).

Because the right eye is connected to the left brain hemisphere then the right eye "sees" what the left brain hemisphere processes. It "sees" the pieces first, sees differences, and sees sequence, structure, etc. If you are left brain hemisphere dominant and right eye dominant, then under stress you will continue to see the detail of things, see the words, the technique, etc.

Under stress, the greatest challenge comes when for example you are left hemispheric dominant and left eye dominant. Now, because the right hemisphere has "quietened" so to speak, the left eye cannot access information as easily. And the non-dominant right eye is also unable to take in information adequately. Thus, one's "sight" becomes challenged. It could be difficult to read and comprehend what you are reading, it could be difficult to see the words on a page, it could be difficult to see sequences, etc. It could be a challenge to take in the whole picture and see the similarities and functions of the right brain hemisphere.

As you will see in Unit 2, you can use Brain Gym® and EFT to help you reclaim an integrated state achieving calm confidence as you face your exams. You can regain access to both brain hemispheres and both eyes, ears, hands and feet for improved learning and expressiveness.

[1] http://www.adaa.org/generalized-anxiety-disorder-gad

[2] www.therapists.com/fundamentals/exam-anxiety

[3] Lipton, Bruce. *The Biology of Belief.* Hay House Publishing, USA. 2008. Pp15-116

[4] Hannaford, Carla, Ph.D. *The Dominance Factor; How Knowing Your Dominant Eye, Ear, Brain, Hand & Foot Can Improve Your Learning.* Salt Lake City, Great River Books. 1997

CHAPTER 4
Am I Alone?

If I Am Not Alone, Then Why Do I Feel That Way?

Believe me – you are not alone! The more I discuss exam anxiety, the more I realize how common it is. One need only research books or visit websites devoted to the topic to find that it is extremely common. Research findings from around the world indicate that the *majority* of students experience it to some degree.

Why do you feel so alone? First, it is possible that you are the kind of person who does not readily discuss the negative experiences on any subject—let alone exam anxiety. You may be reluctant to relate how it affects you, physically, mentally or socially. Without sharing, you will not hear what others might have to say about it. Possibly, it is something you experience once in a while, but not always. However, it is always there, hovering.

Let's repeat that thought –**YOU ARE NOT ALONE!**

Fran Burke, M.Ed.

How often have you sat in a classroom and not been clear on the subject, not quite getting it, with a dozen questions . . . and never asked the teacher those questions. Do you think everyone in the class understood what the teacher was talking about? MOST students are either scared, or ashamed to ask questions. HOW OFTEN DO YOU SEE THE HANDS RAISED WHEN THE TEACHER ASKS, "Are there any questions?" BELIEVE ME — YOU ARE NOT ALONE!

I know I did not admit to it, nor did I experience it every time I took exams. However, when I did have exam anxiety, I felt responsible. I had this belief that there was something wrong with me, and well, I just had to "suck it up." As I reflect on the subject — I recognize that it is also something that we experience for a short period of time — then it is gone . . . UNTIL THE NEXT EXAM.

One reason for overlooking *exam anxiety* in the past was there were few solutions for dealing with it. Today, there are methods to counter the problem (say "Hello" to Brain Gym® and Emotional Freedom Techniques). Education has rarely, if ever, focused on the body or emotions as they relate to the learning process. While this is changing, it has not been fully adopted by educators. With the tools you will acquire here, you will also gain some understanding of the link between the body and brain for optimal learning and performance. Now is the time to break the silence surrounding exam anxiety—to pass on to the next generation the strategies that can nip it in the bud and end, once and for all, the idea that you are alone in your exam anxiety.

As you will see below, research from around the world shows that the majority of students experience some intensity of anxiety around exams.

You Are Not Alone—Some Statistics on Exam Anxiety

That exam anxiety does not distinguish itself with any particular group of students has been verified by the following research studies taken from several different countries.

First, please see what The American Exam Anxieties Association reports:

. . . the majority of students report being more stressed by exams and by schoolwork than by anything else in their lives. About 16-20% of students have high exam anxiety, making this the most prevalent scholastic impairment in our schools today. Another 18% are troubled by moderately-high exam anxiety.[1]

Second, here is an Appraisal of the level of exam anxiety among tertiary education students at Alvan Ikoku Federal College of Education, Owerri, Imo State, Nigeria.

Fran Burke, M.Ed.

Research question: What is the level of exam anxiety amongst students? From Table 1, it can be seen that 90 out of 205 respondents have high anxiety, representing 44% of the sample, while 75 respondents have moderate anxiety.

Finding: you are not alone

Table 1. Level of exam anxiety among students.[2]

Anxiety level	No. of students	Percentage (%)
High	90	44
Moderate	75	36
Low	40	20
Total	205	100

The ChildLine National Exam Stress Survey out of the UK revealed: *that 96% of the 1300 who completed the survey felt anxious about exams and revision, with 59% feeling pressure from their parents to do well . . . 64% saying they have never received any support in dealing with exams.*[3]

Note that one study shows that 64% of students said they received no support for dealing with exam anxiety. This may also be the norm elsewhere. Lacking tools for managing exam anxiety the student was alone with the problem and had to find his or her own solution to the problem.

Worryingly in the survey results, 'some of you said you coped with anxiety by smoking, taking drugs and self-harming. You might feel that this is the only way you can cope with these negative emotions but it doesn't have to be.'

Another alarming statistic reveals that almost half of pupils say they have skipped meals, two- thirds of those surveyed said they have had trouble sleeping and 14% said they have drunk alcohol as a way of dealing with exam anxiety.[4]

You Are Not Alone With Your Exam Anxiety

Much has been written about how to reduce exam anxiety. However, in daily practice, there does not seem to be either the interest, or a voice to deal with it. The subject is rarely discussed. And, when it is, the results are not encouraging. One school system offered up the following information:

Our school board does not have any data regarding exam anxiety specifically. We do have a survey we offer to students regularly and this helps us to determine trends and anxiety may show up on this survey. This survey is a commercial survey, and we purchase it for use with our students.

At the high school level, we do not have a specific program in place. If a student seems to be experiencing anxiety or identifies as having exam anxiety their classroom teacher would work with the guidance counsellor or perhaps the special education people to make modifications for the student to help them be successful. When the students write EQAO provincial exams in grades 3, 6, 9 (math) and 10 (literacy) there are very specific accommodations which can be made but they have to be included in a student's IEP (Individual Education Plan). Each student is treated as an individual and accommodations for exams are made on an individual basis.

Clearly, the school system does not have an understanding of exam anxiety. How can a counsellor aid the student in this area? The source for this information continues:

It is also important to remember that not all courses have formal final exams anymore. Some classes have culminating activities that take place at the end of a course.

LET'S TALK ABOUT COURSES THAT SET EXAMS . . .
I am not aware of any provincial program that offers tools to the teacher for setting up a support system for students with serious exam anxiety.

HAS THE TEACHER REALLY CHECKED THE SYSTEM FOR SUPPORT?
A student does not have to be formally identified as having a disability to obtain help from our school board. Often a teacher can accommodate because they know the students well and know their needs.

THEY ACCOMMODATE? HOW?
It would be interesting to find out how many teachers are actually aware of the extent to which their students experience exam anxiety and the solutions they offer them. Would they have the wherewithal to help them? If exam anxiety is not discussed in teacher's college, pray tell where would they gain knowledge to assist their students?

In university, accommodations can only be made if the student has a psychological assessment and professional diagnosis. If a student has a formal diagnosis, the information can be shared with a post- secondary institution by the student. If they have had a psychological assessment within the last two years, the college or university is able to use this assessment. If it is older than two years, the assessment is no longer valid.

Most colleges and universities have a department to assist students with their accommodations. The students have to make the contact. Sometimes they do this before they attend college/university; that is, while they are still in secondary school.

What follows is an example of the way an Ontario college deals with the problem ... for students living with disabilities looking for help with their academic accommodations:

Fran Burke, M.Ed.

Our friendly, knowledgeable team of accommodation support staff—facilitators, specialists, and administrators—will offer support with academic accommodation and related academic supports and the processes involved with these. Students eligible for Academic Accommodation Support have singular and multiple disabilities, such as learning disabilities, sensory impairments, acquired brain injuries, ADHD, and mental health, medical, and mobility issues.

Students seeking accommodation can contact our main office to register and submit medical documentation. Active students can view their accommodation letters and send electronically to professors, and submit exam or exam booking requests online. Learn more by watching these videos or log in for support.

While it is wonderful that these programs exist *for those who are identified with special needs,* the majority of students who undoubtedly experience varying degrees of exam anxiety do not appear to be offered support.

Is there a need? The answer will astound you!

96% of 1,300 respondents to a ChildLine National Exam Stress Survey said they were affected—exam anxiety is almost epidemic.[5]

How to End Exam Anxiety

Dr. Luisa Dillner, writer and doctor reports in The Guardian:

. . . research shows that highly anxious students score 12 percentile points lower than averagely anxious ones, and parental pressure increases the risk of children feeling physical symptoms of anxiety and distracted thinking in exams.[6]

As a child of parents who were educators, a student of 18+ years, and an educator, it has been my experience that action is not being taken.

So is it possible to halt, or at a minimum, reduce exam anxiety? Yes it is! Let us begin by taking a look at solutions to exam anxiety.

REMEMBER: YOU ARE NOT ALONE.

[1] American Test Anxieties Association. http://www.amtaa.org/
[2] Alvan Ikoku Federi College of Education, Owerri, Imo State, Nigeria
       http://www.netjournals.org/pdf/AERJ/2014?1/12-011pdf
[3] The ChildLine National Exam Stress Survey
       http://www.mentalhealthy.co.uk/news/321-pressure-of-exams-causing-worrying-levels-of-anxiety-in-students.html.
[4] http://www.mentalhealthy.co.uk/news/321-pressure-of-exams-causing-worrying-level
[5] The ChildLine National Exam Stress Survey

Fran Burke, M.Ed.

http://www.mentalhealthy.co.uk/news/321-pressure-of- exams-causing-worrying-levels-of-anxiety-in-students.html

[6] Dillner, Luisa, Dr.

http://www.theguardian.com/lifeandstyle/2015/may/10/can-i-do-anything-to-stop-exam-anxiety-exams-fear

UNIT 2: SHORT-TERM SOLUTIONS FOR EXAM ANXIETY

CHAPTER 5
Calm Your Anxiety with Brain Gym® Activities

Please note: if you need to reduce exam anxiety right now, please go directly to **Part Two** of this chapter where the Brain Gym® activities are described. You can return to **Part One** later.

The effectiveness of practicing Brain Gym® activities for reducing exam anxiety is all about *countering an involuntary action (survival response) with purposeful mental and physical action.* In the previous chapters, you read about some of what happens in the brain-body system when the survival response takes place, and how it can affect you behaviorally, cognitively, emotionally, chemically and neurologically.

Brain Gym® activities can be used at the time you feel anxious and are experiencing this survival response. Use them when you are preparing for an exam, or on the day of the exam, or immediately before or even during the exam. The more you practice them and incorporate them into daily routine, the more you can face life in an integrated state. That means easier learning and better expression.

Fran Burke, M.Ed.

PART ONE: About Brain Gym®¹*

Created by educational pioneer Paul Dennison, Brain Gym® is a program made up of a series of twenty-six movements which theoretically help you be in a relaxed, receptive and expressive state to learn. These movements engage the side-to-side, up and down, and front and back dimensions of the brain-body system. They reportedly enhance communication, organization, focus and comprehension. When we are in a relaxed state, optimal learning is possible. However, when stressed, the system is not integrated—learning becomes challenged. In this stressed state, not only can it be difficult to receive and retain information, it can also be difficult to express what learning has taken place. Under stress the brain-body system may be in a state of fight-flight-freeze and the individual may react solely by reflex.

Dennison was young when he discovered that certain types of movement helped him overcome some of his own, unique, learning challenges. Later, as an educator and reading specialist, he continued to research. He explored and incorporated body movements in order to help his students excel in their studies. Through this extensive investigation and his own work with students, Dennison developed a deep and unique understanding of the importance of how moving with intention could bring about optimal learning. Since its inception,

Dennison's Brain Gym® program has contributed to advancements in learning of students around the world.

After ground-breaking research in the 1960's, Dennison developed his movement-based program. Since then, Dennison and his wife, Gail Dennison, have incorporated Brain Gym® into the field of movement-based learning known as Educational Kinesiology.[2] This has become a worldwide network of individuals dedicated to empowering all ages to re-claim the joy of living through movement-based programs. As indicated on its official website www.braingym.org, the Brain Gym® educational model is designed to:

- promote play and the joy of learning
- draw out and honor innate intelligence
- build awareness regarding the value of movement in daily life
- emphasize the ability to notice and respond to movement-based needs
- encourage self-responsibility
- leave each participant appreciated and valued
- empower each participant to better take charge of his own learning

Brain Gym is a registered trademark of the Educational Kinesiology Foundation, Ventura, CA, USA 93023

- encourage creativity and self-expression
- inspire an appreciation of music, physical education and the fine arts

Some Brain Gym® activities may help calm your system, bring it out of the fight-flight-freeze mode and into a state of prepared learning. These same activities may help you relax in order to do your best on exams.

The seven Brain Gym® activities described below are helpful in relaxing the common state known as "butterflies" and in retrieving information when we sit at an exam. They are truly ideal exercises before an exam. Please note that while these activities can help you become calm and confident, they represent a small fraction of the number of beneficial activities Brain Gym® offers, and their unique applications.

Except for the first activity, *Sip Water*, these activities can be done standing, sitting or lying down.

So that you can get started right away to achieve the calm confidence you are looking for around your exams, **Part Two** explains how to do the activities and some of the benefits people experience from doing them. Start with the first activity and work through all seven. Simply notice the change in how they affect you. Notice your breathing and when you catch yourself holding your breath while doing these activities, engage your breath again.

The best way to recognize when these following activities are effective is by "noticing." What do you notice about yourself before using them? Are you breathing shallowly? Are your muscles tense or relaxed? How do you feel? Then, after completing the activities, notice again. What changed? How are your beliefs, thoughts, behaviors, emotions and body different? Become aware of how they benefitted you.

Noticing:

As you go about practicing these Brain Gym® activities, the act of *noticing* is most important.

According to Dennison, "Noticing is a process of focusing one's attention in the present and paying attention to how we do what we do. We consciously *notice* how we observe, becoming aware of the ways we accumulate information through our visual, auditory and other senses."[3]

As you practice these activities, *notice* any change in how you sense things, how you feel emotionally and physically, and how your thinking might change. According to your experience and what you ***notice***, make the adjustments necessary to achieve the goal you wish to achieve. Developing your *noticing* skills allows you to achieve your goals more optimally.

In the instance of exam anxiety, practice the Brain Gym® activities, *notice* how they help bring about the calm and confidence you are after, and the clarity of thought. Adjust how long you do each one according to your need. Choose some activities over others if that feels most beneficial. Use noticing to make that choice. By so doing you are taking personal responsibility and may also achieve optimal learning.

Practicing the following Brain Gym® activities is about countering an involuntary action (anxiety) with purposeful mental and physical action.

A REMINDER: please be aware that there are times when one needs professional help. This book is simply not enough. When anxiety is affecting other parts of your life and the techniques discussed here do not provide the calm and confidence you are striving for at exam time, perhaps a psychologist or other mental health professional would be better suited to help your situation. Also, if appropriate, inquire if your school has counseling services.

PART TWO: The Brain Gym® Activities

Prepare Yourself before Starting the Brain Gym® Activities

First, take time to imagine yourself at the exam you are about to take. Imagine how you would like to **BE** while writing your exam. *This is most important to do before you do the Brain Gym® Activities.*

What has your exam experience been like in the past? For example, do you freeze and become unable to think during the exam? Or do you have distracting thoughts that keep you from focusing on your exam? Do you shake or have a pounding heart? Or, do you replay your past negative experiences in your mind when you have another exam to write? Think about what you have experienced.

NOW STOP! It is important to stop replaying the negative experiences in your mind's eye. Chances are this is what you think about when you hear an exam being announced or anticipate writing your next exam.

Instead, **IMAGINE** how you **WANT** your exam experience to be. Play this experience in your mind. For example, imagine *feeling* confident. How does that *feel* in your body and head?

Imagine how you see yourself during your exam. See yourself sitting confidently, smiling as you come to each question, happy to show what you know about the subject on which you are being tested. Imagine yourself coming to a question that may stump you. See yourself letting it go until you have finished all those that you can answer quickly and easily. Then go back to the one that stumps you. You may find that the answer has come to your mind or that you have found the answer in an exam question. In your imagination, take a brief moment to look around you at the other students who are writing their exams. As you do, feel how relaxed and confident you are. How easy it is for you to see and hear the sights and sounds around you. Imagine how clear your thinking is and how easy it is for you to answer the questions. Know that you have studied everything necessary to do well on your exam. In fact, you are *excited* to show yourself and the teacher what you know.

Now, it's your turn. In the space below, write out what you wish your experience to be. Role-play it! Imagine it! Do everything you can to make your desired experience of writing your exam as **REAL** as you possibly can. This is your **GOAL**. This is your **INTENTION**. Whenever you start replaying past negative experiences, acknowledge that is happening. Say **STOP!** Start to **IMAGINE** what you **WANT**.

In the space below write, "During my exam I want to be:

-
-
-
-
-
-
-

Now imagine yourself being that way. Role-play how you wish to be.

Now it's time to do the Brain Gym® activities below.

After you have completed the Brain Gym® movements, replay your GOAL in your mind again and notice the shift that has taken place. Is it easier to be the new you at exam time? Repeat as you need. Know that you will experience your exam in a positive new way.

The first four activities are grouped together and are given the title **PACE**. While each activity can be practiced independently of the others to calm the system, when practiced together they are not only most effective, but also may help bring about optimal learning through movement with intention.

What You Might Expect from Doing PACE.[4] – The four activities below

PACE stands for a series of four activities which when done together help integrate the brain-body system for optimal learning. For best results one can incorporate **PACE** daily. In fact, it can be done many times per day. It can be very helpful to start the day with this activity and to get in the practice of doing it before learning in the classroom and before sitting down to study and even as an activity to do as a break from studying. As well, one can choose to do **PACE** before starting to study for an exam and before writing it. **PACE** can be calming, allowing you to focus on the task at hand.

PACE stands for Positive, Active, Clear and Energetic. For best results, it is practiced in a reverse sequence starting with **E**, then **C, A** and finally **P**.:

E. Sip Water - Energetic
C. Brain Buttons - Clear
A. The Cross Crawl - Active
P. Hook-Ups - Positive

To start, it is recommended that each activity in **PACE** (Brain Buttons, Cross Crawl and Hook-Ups) take about thirty seconds. As you practice, you may feel your system needs more than thirty seconds for one or more of the activities. When you notice this, take as much time as your body indicates rather than feel you must limit the activity to thirty seconds. Also, as you make **PACE** a regular practice, you may find that there are some of movements which help you feel more relaxed than others. When you discover these, you might want to use them independent of the **PACE** routine, too.

How to do the PACE Activities

Energetic

Sip Water

Sipping rather than gulping water is the most effective way to restore hydration. Dr. Paul Dennison states that "As with light rain falling on dry ground, water is best absorbed by the body when taken in frequent small amounts."[5]

Fran Burke, M.Ed.

What You Might Expect From Sipping Water

Sipping water is an effective way to restore hydration to the body. In *Smart Moves, Why Learning Is Not All in Your Head,* biologist and educator, Carla Hannaford explains that *"water . . . makes up eighty percent of our body weight at birth and seventy percent of an adult's body weight . . . Our bodily systems are electrical.*

Ultimately, it is the electrical transmissions within the nervous system that make us sensing, learning, thinking, and acting organisms. Water, the universal solvent, is essential for these electrical transmissions and for maintaining the electrical potential within our bodies."[6]

As well, being hydrated helps with the efficient electrical and chemical action between the brain and the rest of the nervous system. It can enhance the efficient storage and retrieval of information, improve all academic skills and is vital before taking an exam and at other possible times when stress is expected. It can help with concentration, improved mental and physical coordination, release of stress and enhanced communication and social skills.

Not only does stress cause the brain-body system to require additional water, but coffee, black tea and other caffeinated drinks cause the body to lose water. If students are in the habit of drinking these beverages while preparing for exams, it is important to increase water intake. No other beverage benefits the body as much as water. There is no replacement for it.

Under normal conditions, Hannaford recommends a person drink three ounces of water per pound of body weight (about a quart per one hundred pounds) with this amount being doubled or tripled during stressful times.[7] If in doubt, always consult your medical doctor.

2. Clear

Brain Buttons[8]

Stimulate the Brain Buttons by forming a U shape with one hand by placing your thumb and index finger in the soft depressions just below your collarbones and to each side of your sternum. Place your other hand over your navel. Rub the Brain Buttons for twenty or thirty seconds. However, if they are tender, you may want to take a little more time to rub them until the tenderness decreases or disappears. With your head and lower hand held still, move your eyes slowly back and forth from the left and right along a horizontal line. Switch your hands and repeat the activity."

What You Might Expect From Doing Brain Buttons

Doing Brain Buttons may help you with your reading. They may be beneficial when our eyes lose their focus. You may find that you can move your eyes more easily across the page and keep your place while reading. You may also find that they can help you with physical balance, increased energy level and neck and shoulder relaxation - areas of the body that can become tight when anxious.

The Cross Crawl[9]

Stand comfortably and reach across the midline of your body while moving one arm and its opposite leg alternately. Then move the other arm and leg. Rhythmically touch each elbow or hand to the opposite knee. Feel the contralateral movement as it originates from the core of your body.

Be sure that you are touching opposite knee to opposite elbow. If touching opposite elbow to opposite knee is challenging to start, then touch opposite hand to opposite knee and work up to getting the elbow and knee to touch later.

What You Might Expect From Doing "The Cross Crawl"

The Cross Crawl may help with spelling, writing, listening, attention, reading and comprehension and finally with breathing and stamina. These may all be helpful when sitting down to write an exam!

4. Positive

"Hook-ups"[10]

Part 1: Start by crossing your ankles. Then, extend your arms in front of you and cross one wrist over the other. Face the palms to each other and interlace your fingers. Now, draw your clasped hands up towards your chest. While holding for a minute or more, breathe in slowly. You can choose to have your eyes open or closed. As you inhale, touch the tip of your tongue to the roof of your mouth at the hard palate (just behind your teeth), and relax your tongue on exhalation.

Part II: When you choose, uncross your arms and legs and put your fingertips together in front of your chest. Continue to breathe deeply for another minute and hold the tip of your tongue on the roof of your mouth when you inhale.

What You Might Expect From Doing Hook-Ups

Hook-ups have value in becoming centered. They may help you feel more grounded, more organized, controlled in your breathing, and calm you. They may help improve listening and speaking, self-control plus feel comfort in any environment. They pay dividends when sitting in the examination room waiting for the exam to start.

N.B. *If you are at all unsteady on your feet, or your balance while standing is not that sound sit down. This will give you greater security during the exercise.*

Additional Brain Gym® Activities for Relaxing the Butterflies and Retrieving Information

"The Positive Points"[11]

Think of something that ordinarily causes you stress, like an upcoming exam. While doing so, like a butterfly wing touching your forehead, lightly hold the two points halfway between your hairline and your eyebrows with the fingertips of your two hands. In other words, the area just above the center of each eye. Use only enough pressure to pull taut any slackness of the skin. A slight pulse may be felt at these points. That is just fine. Depending on the severity of the problem, continue to hold the points for about twenty seconds or up to ten minutes.

What You Might Expect From Doing "Positive Points"

Positive Points may help reduce stress, help relax you, lead you from an anxious moment, allowing you to regroup. They may help you release a temporary memory block – that "the answer's on the tip of my tongue" situation. They may help you improve your ability to organize, study and memorize and be confident at exam time.

"Lazy Eights"[12]

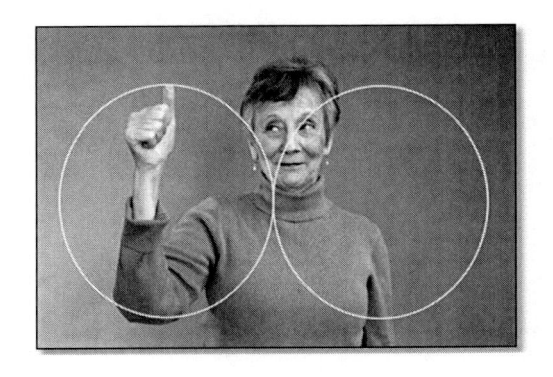

In the air in front of you, draw with one thumb a large eight lying on its side. As you move your thumb, track it with both eyes keeping your head still. Always move counter-clockwise. In other words, start on the left side first – up, over, and around – and then clockwise on the right side, up, over, and around. Do this three times. Then switch hands and move in the same pattern three more times (always moving counter-clockwise on the left side first). Lastly, clasp your hands together, crossing your thumbs and draw the same pattern three times with both hands.

What You Might Expect From Doing the "Lazy Eights"

This activity encourages the coordination of the eyes for crossing the visual midline without interruption thus building eye-movement skills within the left, right, and central visual fields. In other words, there is a definite midpoint and distinct left and right areas, joined by a continuous line. As the eyes follow the flowing movement of the hands, they learn to focus together for binocular vision.

"Earth Buttons"

Rest two fingertips (usually the pointing and middle fingers) under your lower lip. Place the palm of the other hand over your navel with the fingertips pointing down along the midline. Your chin will automatically tuck itself in. Picture that you are breathing air up the center of your body. Look down and let your eyes track a vertical line. It can be a line from floor to ceiling or a corner of the room. As you do this, feel your grounded connection to the earth and hold the points for four to six complete breaths. Change hands and repeat.

What You Might Expect From Doing "Earth Buttons"

Earth Buttons may help you to improve your eye-teaming ability, improved centering, and depth perception. They may help with near-to-far visual skills e.g. looking back and forth from the paper on your desk the blackboard. Earth Buttons may help alleviate mental fatigue and maintain good posture plus a sense of being grounded.

CONCLUSION

The Brain Gym® activities shared with you in this chapter can support you in feeling calm and confident on exam day. Any exam day! Remember, to imagine how you want your exam experience to be and hold that picture in your mind before you do the Brain Gym® movements and even while you are doing them. Then as mentioned above, all but the first one can be done standing, sitting or lying down. They can be practiced almost anywhere there is a safe space in which to do them. Again, some are perfect to practice while waiting for the exam to start, or while pondering material you have studied. There are times when the stress is so severe it is difficult to even read the instructions, much less comprehend them. Use some of the Brain Gym® exercises you have learned, relax and ace that exam.

One more thing: keep in mind that Brain Gym® has much more to offer any student in learning and optimum performance. Should you work with these programs, enjoy them and would like to learn more, look for a Brain Gym® instructor in your area. On the other hand, if they do not bring about the calm confidence that you want, it may be that you will need other Brain Gym® practices to achieve those results.

[1] www.braingym.org
[2] www.braingym.org
[3] Dennison, Paul E. and Gail E. Dennison. *Brain Gym® 101 Balance for Daily Life*. Ventura, Edu Kinesthetics, Inc. 2007. P. 5.
[4] Dennison, Paul E. and Gail E. Dennison. *Brain Gym® 101 Balance for Daily Life*. Ventura, Edu-Kinesthetics, Inc. 2007. pp. 12-13.

[5] Dennison, Paul E. and Gail E. Dennison. *Brain Gym® Teacher's Edition; The Companion Guide to Brain Gym®: Simple Activities for Whole Brain Learning.* Ventura, Ca. Hearts at Play Inc. 2010. P. 54

[6] Hannaford, Carla. *Smart Moves; Why Learning Is Not All In Your Head.* Salt Lake City, Great River Books. 2005. Pp. 150-151.

[7] Hannaford, Carla. *Smart Moves; Why Learning Is Not All In Your Head.* Salt Lake City, Great River Books. 2005. Pp. 150-151.

[8] Dennison, Paul E. and Gail E. Dennison. *Brain Gym® 101 Balance for Daily Life.* Ventura, Edu- Kinesthetics, Inc. 2007. P. 62.

[9] Dennison, Paul E. and Gail E. Dennison. *Brain Gym®101 Balance for Daily Life.* Ventura, Edu- Kinesthetics, Inc. 2007. P. 59.

[10] Dennison, Paul E. and Gail E. Dennison. *Brain Gym® 101 Balance for Daily Life.* Ventura, Edu-Kinesthetics, Inc. 2007. P64

[11] Dennison, Paul E. and Gail E. Dennison. *Brain Gym® 101 Balance for Daily Life.* Ventura, Edu- Kinesthetics, Inc. 2007. P64

[12] Dennison, Paul E. and Gail E. Dennison. *Brain Gym® 101 Balance for Daily Life.* Ventura, Edu- Kinesthetics, Inc. 2007. 60

[13] Dennison, Paul E. and Gail E. Dennison. *Brain Gym® 101 Balance for Daily Life.* Ventura, Edu- Kinesthetics, Inc. 2007. P. 62

CHAPTER 6
Calm Your Anxiety with Emotional Freedom Techniques[1]

What are Emotional Freedom Techniques?

The Emotional Freedom Techniques, EFT or Tapping, falls under the umbrella of Energy Psychology. It is a powerful technique for personal transformation by combining the five-thousand year-old eastern medical tradition of acupressure or acupuncture and western talk-therapy. It has been found to be highly effective in managing both emotional and physical health. Considering the physical and mental- emotional aspects of exam anxiety, it can be highly effective in addressing them. It is both a physical and mental approach to dealing with anxiety. Like Brain Gym®, EFT is another tool to be used to *counter a reflex caused by anxiety through focused mental and physical action.*

Be aware there are times when you may require professional help. This book may not enough. If anxiety is affecting other parts of your life, and the techniques discussed here do not work to accomplish the calm, the confidence you seek, please consider contacting a psychologist or other mental health professional for help. Ask if your school has counseling services.

EFT is easy to learn. It can help you deal with the negative emotions and physical discomfort of exam anxiety. Once you have been able to release those conditions, through EFT, new insights and understanding will emerge and you will approach exams and other challenges with a new calm and confidence.

Why do EFT?

EFT is a very quick method of reducing anxiety. By tapping on points shown on the diagram below you can greatly reduce the survival reaction. "Acupoint tapping sends signals directly to the stress centers of the mid-brain, that part of the brain not mediated by the frontal lobes (the thinking part, active in talk-therapy). Because EFT simultaneously accesses stress on physical and emotional levels, EFT gives you the best of both worlds, body and mind, like getting a massage during a psychotherapy session.

In fact, it is EFT's ability to calm the amygdala (an almond-shaped structure in each of the temporal lobes of the brain that initiates your body's fight-flight-freeze response) that makes it so powerful. By reducing stress, EFT helps with many problems—exam anxiety being one of them. There are other ways it may be used—in sports performance, business and financial pressure and body discomfort. When you reduce stress in one area of your life, there is often a beneficial effect in other areas.

It is remarkable that tapping sends a message to the amygdala, signaling that all is well, it is safe to relax. This has the effect of disengaging whatever issue you are tapping on from the body's stress response (fight-flight-freeze) with immediate results both emotionally and even physically. How helpful this is when you are faced with exam anxiety.

How Do You Do EFT?

As mentioned previously, EFT is a form of psychological acupressure; it is based on the same energy meridian system used in traditional acupuncture. This tradition has been practiced to alleviate health issues for over five thousand years.

In the tapping portion of EFT, you simply tap with two, or three fingertips on specified meridian points mostly located on the head and chest. They are identified on the illustration below. Most people do their own tapping. Some clients will have a practitioner do the required tapping.

Meridians are energy channels that transport life energy or Chi/Qi throughout the body. Energy meridian points are at the ends of these energy meridians and are located just beneath the surface of the skin. They respond to touch.

Tapping Locations & Technique

There are four basic aspects to learn in order to use EFT:
1) Learning the *Tapping Points;*
2) Identifying the *Subjective Units of Distress* of an **Issue** to be tapped on;
3) Creating the *Set-up Statement* and *Reminder Phrase;*
4) Learning the *Tapping Sequence.*

1. EFT Tapping Points

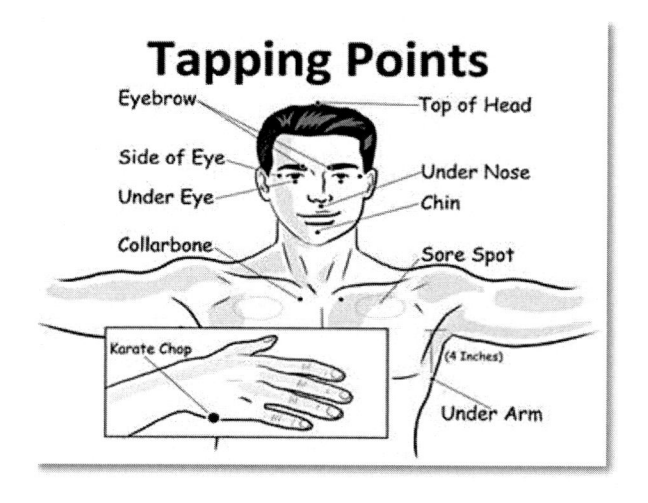

Tapping Points
- Eyebrow
- Top of Head
- Side of Eye
- Under Nose
- Under Eye
- Chin
- Collarbone
- Sore Spot
- Karate Chop
- (4 Inches)
- Under Arm

KC = Karate Chop
EB = Eye Brow
SE = Side of the Eye
UE = Under the Eye
UN = Under the Nose
CH = Chin
CB = Collar Bone
UA = Under the Arm
TH = Top of Head

2. Subjective Units of Distress or SUDS:

- You need to identify a most pressing *Issue*. What is causing you the discomfort or pain? Is it your thoughts, your feelings, your behavior, a physical discomfort? If there is more than one, choose one and determine the **Subjective Units of Distress or SUDS.**
- To determine the **Subjective Units of Distress,** think about how intense your issue is. On a scale of 0 – 10: 0 = no issue at all and 10 = the most distress you can experience. Choose the number to represent how intense you feel the physical/emotional pain or discomfort.
- You will use this measure to determine the effectiveness of your tapping. The purpose will be to bring this **SUDS** level from 0 - 3. When it is at 0, or close to it, you will have overcome the issue by reducing its intensity. This can be

accompanied by a corresponding calmer, less stressful view of the situation.

3. Create a Set-up Statement and a Reminder Phrase re: your most pressing Issue.

- The *Set-up Statement* includes the following phrase: *"Even though state your Issue here clearly, I deeply and completely love and accept myself."*

  Some examples of *Set-up Statements* for exam anxiety could be:

  - "Even though I feel this level 8 anxious feeling about this exam because I have to get an A, I deeply and completely love and accept myself."
  - "Even though what I hear the teacher say about this exam really scares me, I deeply and completely love and accept myself."
  - "Even though I have this level ten fear that I will lose my friends if I fail, I am a great kid and I will do my best."
  - "Even though I feel this level 6 anxiety because I don't know if I have studied enough, I am still okay, believe in myself and will do my best."
  - "Even though I can't stop worrying about how I did on my exam and I keep going over and over the questions

in my mind, I deeply and completely love and accept myself."

- The *Reminder Phrase* comes from the *Set-Up Statement.* It is the *Issue* statement. For example, from the **Set-up Statements** above the *Reminder Phrases* are:

  - "This level 8 anxious feeling; I have to get an A."
  - "What I hear the teacher say about the exam really scares me."
  - "This level 10 fear I will lose my friends if I fail."
  - "This level 6 anxiety. I don't know if I have studied enough."
  - "I can't stop worrying about how I did on my exam and I keep going over and over the questions in my mind."

4. The Tapping Sequence: Once you have determined your **Issue** and the **SUDS** level, it is time to do some tapping. When tapping:

- **Tap** (solidly but gently using the tips of two to three fingers) about 5 – 7 times on the Karate Chop point while saying the *Set-Up Statement.* Then repeat tapping on the KC point while also repeating the *Set-Up Statement* two more times (for a total of 15-21 taps and three *Set-Up Statements*).

- **Then** tap about 5-7 times on each of the points while repeating the ***Reminder Phrase***. It is okay to tap on both sides of the body, on only one side or even switch sides.
- After you have tapped the full cycle of points once or twice repeating the ***Reminder Phrase*** at each point (from the EB point to the TH point), stop, take a deep breath and determine the **SUDS** level of your issue.
- Hopefully, the level of intensity has dropped. If it has not dropped to a level from 0 – 3, repeat the process one more time.
- Continue to tap, stop, assess until your feeling is no higher than a 3 and preferably at 0.

Please notice that except for the TH point, these tapping points proceed down the body. That is, each tapping point is below the one before it. That should make it a snap to memorize. The sequence is not critical. You can tap the points in any order and sequence, just so long as all the points are covered. It is just easier to go from top to bottom to make sure you remember to do them all.

Three Standards of Tapping

These levels of tapping have been identified and named by Nancy Forrester, CEO of the National EFT Training Institute in

Ontario, Canada (www.neftti.com). She identifies these levels based on needs and the depth required in order to resolve issues.

1. The Bronze Standard can help you reduce tension by simply tapping. Sometimes all that is needed is simply tapping on the points. It may be that you do not have the time, or place to do anything more, but desire to reduce the tension you are feeling. For example, you are sitting at the exam and the anxiety is welling up. You cannot talk and tap - so you simply tap. Or, perhaps you freeze and cannot remember what you had studied. Simply sit back and tap. Here is how:

- Start by tapping on the KC point 5 – 7 times and then repeating this two more times for a total of 15 – 21 taps.
- Then, proceed to tap 5 – 7 times on each of the remaining points starting with the EB point and ending with the TH point. Take a deep breath and assess the intensity of your thoughts, feelings or physical tension. That is it! Repeat as needed.

2. The Silver Standard can help you work at a deeper level by following a script that has been pre-written to address a certain issue. Here are scripts that may address one or more of your issues concerning exam anxiety.

- Even though *I have this level 8 fear of my upcoming exam,* I deeply and completely love and accept myself.
- Even though *I feel sick to my stomach thinking about this exam,* I deeply and completely love and accept myself.
- Even though *I don't feel ready to write this exam and I want to stay home,* I deeply and completely love and accept myself.
- Even though *I don't know what I will do if I don't pass this exam,* I deeply and completely love and accept myself.
- Even though *I am afraid my parents will ground me if I don't get an A,* I deeply and completely love and accept myself.
- Even though *I can't stop worrying about the answers I wrote on my exam and I feel powerless to make any changes now,* I deeply and completely love and accept myself."
  - Remember to identify a most pressing **Issue**. In this case it is exam anxiety. Choose a script that most closely matches your Issue.
  - Determine the **Subjective Units of Distress** or **SUDS**. Think about how intense your anxiety is. On a scale of 0 – 10: 0 = no anxiety at all and 10 = the most intense anxiety you could ever experience. Choose the number to represent how intense you feel the physical/emotional anxiety.
  - Start to tap following a **Script** that includes a **Set-up Statement** and a **Reminder Phrase**. (The bolded phrases

are your reminder phrases.)
- After a round or two of tapping, assess your **SUDS** level again. If your distress is not yet from 3 – 0, repeat the process again. Your aim is to reduce the distress to a minimum of 3 and preferably 0.
- Repeat as needed.

3. The Gold Standard is the next level of tapping. It is most helpful when you need to get more specific about your particular situation before you can experience relief. This level requires professional training available from the National EFT Training Institute www.NeftTI.com. Or you could work with a certified EFT practitioner, like myself fran@howtoend examanxiety.com. At times, you may need expert assistance in resolving issues too challenging to deal with on your own. They may be to too painful or scary to face alone. These may include: phobias; traumas of different intensities including Post Traumatic Stress Disorder (PTSD). It could be addictions.

The Gold Level Tapping could be your answer if you have tried the Bronze and Silver Levels with little or no progress in overcoming exam anxiety. Memories, thoughts, beliefs, behaviors or events from your past could be holding you back.

Fran Burke, M.Ed.

In EFT We Start with Negative Emotions First and End with Affirmations

Negative feelings and memories which have not been dealt with (or neutralized) are alive and well either in your subconscious or your body. It is very common to for us to avoid dealing with them. This avoidance may take any number of forms. For example, you may try to bury them by pushing them out of your mind when they surface, or busy yourself to keep your attention away from them. You may numb yourself with alcohol, drugs or in other ways. The fact is that until you neutralize your negative emotions through EFT, they can continue to interfere in your life. For example: they may surface unexpectedly when a memory is triggered; prevent or disturb your sleep; keep you from accomplishing your goals; interfere with concentration; drain your energy or even promote disease.

When the negative feelings, behaviors and beliefs are addressed and neutralized, we achieve freedom. One tool to accomplish this freedom is the Emotional *Freedom* Techniques. With this technique emotional charges are neutralized. They can no longer haunt you, sap energy or promote ill health.

Positive affirmations are wonderful if a negative emotion, behavior or belief has been cleared. However, stating affirmations about yourself when your "little voice" is negating the affirmation, can have a reverse effect on what you are trying to accomplish. Often we choose an affirmation to counter something that we wish to change in our life. For example - you might choose an affirmation like: "I always do well on exams." If this is a true statement, then use it. However, if it is not a true statement and you keep repeating this affirmation, you might hear a small voice doubting the thought. This could compound the problem. So, first clear the mind by accepting reality: (i.e. "Even though I don't do well on exams, I deeply and completely love and accept myself.") then use the positive affirmations. ("Even though I have not done well on exams in the past, I choose to do what it takes to do better or to improve my results.")

EFT may help overcome exam anxiety on many levels. If you have concerns about your performance, the **Bronze Level of Tapping** has been found to be a good tension eraser.

If you have a specific concern about an exam you may want to try the **Silver Level of Tapping** using some scripts that have been designed for such problems. The scripts may be found at website www.nomoreexamanxiety.com.

If the Bronze and Sliver tapping fail to provide relief from exam anxiety, please contact me at fran@howtoendexamanxiety.com for the Gold Level of Tapping. We can explore more deeply what might be causing your anxiety, and lack of a calm confidence at exam time.

Brain Gym® and EFT for reducing Exam Anxiety:

You might be wondering, "How do I know when to use Brain Gym® and when to use EFT?" There are no hard and fast rules. Both systems help reduce the fight-flight-freeze response. In its simplest form, Brain Gym® can help remove you from the fight-flight-freeze response, and integrate your body-brain system for ease of learning and expression.

EFT can help you do the same by tapping out the thoughts, behavior, and beliefs from your past that contribute to the exam anxiety. They complement each other for best results. EFT and Brain Gym® complement each other in producing results. ***They both counter the involuntary fight-flight-freeze reflex using voluntary thought and action.***

Noticing is a good place to start. Notice what is causing you to feel tense. Is it that you need water? Where are you holding your tension? In the case of exam anxiety, is it your thoughts about the exam that are causing the anxiety? Perhaps you feel overwhelmed, disorganized, unfocused, unprepared, afraid of what will happen if you do not do well, afraid of letting yourself down, etc. Any of these can cause you to experience physical tensions. Perhaps you get a tension headache, your shoulders are up around your ears, your stomach is tight, you cannot focus your eyes, you find it hard to concentrate, you find it difficult to think or to hear, etc. Be aware of your mental and physical states. Remember to keep sipping water to keep yourself hydrated. Then, start with EFT or Brain Gym®, the one that calls to you most strongly at the time. Take time to notice how you feel afterwards. If you have experienced relief, great! If not, assess where you are. If you have done some Brain Gym® movements, you may want to do them all again, or hold some of the movements longer, e.g. Hook-ups, Positive Points or Brain Buttons. You may want to take a longer time to do The Cross Crawl or Lazy 8's. Use noticing. If you have used Bronze Level Tapping, take some time to tap again. With Silver Level Tapping, you may need to change the script. You may start with Brain Gym® and finish with Tapping. You may start with Tapping and finish with Brain Gym®.

[1] www.emofree.com

[2] www.neftti.com

UNIT 3: LONG-TERM SOLUTIONS

What follows are some effective long-term solutions for overcoming exam anxiety - long-term solutions because they can take time to learn and develop. When practiced routinely they will become second nature. They are actions to help you structure your life for success and include: *"growth mindset;"* *goal setting, study skills; learning methods,* and *habits for self-care.* It might be useful to scan these pages and check off those things you already practice. Then, select one long-term program that you think will most assist you in achieving your goal and start using it. When you are comfortable using it, choose another that will further help you. By practicing these long-term solutions doggedly, constantly, you help yourself stay in balance.

CHAPTER 7
Mindset

"Success consists of going from failure to failure without loss of enthusiasm."
Winston Churchill

What is A Growth Mindset?

The above quote expresses success in such a very special way. Many successful people, e.g. - Thomas Edison, Henry Ford, and Michael Jordan, all discussed their successes. However, they were just as quick to relate the number of times they failed before they succeeded. According to psychologist, Dr. Carol Dweck, this is the **"growth mindset"**[1] in action. She coined this term out of her extensive research to find out how people coped with failure. She found that many people were not discouraged by failure at all. In fact, even when they "failed" they considered that they were **learning**. They somehow knew that their intellectual and physical skills could be developed through **effort**. They felt they were getting smarter and more knowledgeable even when they failed at some task. They accepted failure and learned from it. Much of the drive to meet challenges came from knowing that they could grow. They would succeed!

Dweck coined another term- an opposite term - **"fixed mindset"**[2]. Dweck used this for people who believed that IQ is carved in stone[3]: you were smart or you were not. She further found that those with a fixed mindset believed failure meant you were not smart. And, if you could avoid failure at all costs, you could stay smart. She discovered that many believed struggles, mistakes, and perseverance were not suffered by smart people. There is evidence to the contrary!

There are consequences for these opposite mindsets. They can determine how you will act in life, the chances you will or will not take, and the goals you may pursue.

With a **"growth mindset"** you believe your ability is different from everyone else; however, you realize that effort, training and development will help you attain your goal.

How Does Having a Growth Mindset Relate to Reducing Exam Anxiety?

Fear of exams may be greatly reduced by taking the position that exam results are not a reflection of who you are, your intelligence, your self-worth, or of your ability. Rather it provides feedback on how well you understood or "knew" the material on the examination.

You understand the consequences of a poor result and know how to respond accordingly. That is, you can use your back-up plan. You know you can recover from a poor showing. Results may not always be positive; you had considered such an event, and now take it as a challenge - an opportunity to rise to the occasion.

The sooner you adopt a **"growth mindset,"** the quicker you will be proactive in your studies, developing ways to achieve confidence at exam time. Do your very best to prepare for any type of evaluation using the knowledge, skills and strategies you have learned in this book. Your confidence will soar. **"Growth mindset"** will take you to the next level.

It is readily apparent that the stakes are higher if your exam mark determines whether or not you will be accepted into a desired program. The stakes are even higher if you do not have a financial safety net. Without such support, of course there is more pressure to succeed at exam time. **"Growth mindset"** will earn you that success.

One way to help is to have a back-up plan—a plan that is the next best thing to your first plan. Back-up plans have the benefit of helping to reduce the anxiety and pressure of exams while at the same time helping you shine at exam time.

According to Dweck, adopting a "growth mindset" can promote greater opportunity to grow, to learn, enjoy and seek challenges. Define your successes in **learning and growth**. You are not trying to prove anything. A side benefit is increased self-confidence. This mindset provides the resilience to spring back from setbacks, and meet and master challenges. Be thoughtful and responsive to both positive and negative feedback—you will find a message in both, and understand required action(s). *Remember neither your ability nor intelligence are cast in stone. Focus on what needs improvement. Resist fear of failure.*

A recent finding in neuroscience is of the ability of the brain to grow due to changes in attention, effort, movement and engagement. The brain is like a muscle. The more you challenge it, the more you develop your mental capacity. As it develops, problems you once thought difficult become easy. So, everyone can actually increase their intelligence and can work on their defects. By continuing to assess a situation and apply new learning, we may ultimately achieve success. Geniuses have to work at their tasks.

As mentioned earlier, there had been the belief that each person is born with a set *intelligence quotient,* ability and character, and that they could not be improved. Having such beliefs, we may feel very intimidated by anything that threatens that identity. Being resilient means you understand that failure is a part of learning and that failure is also a teacher. ***Again—failure does not define you.*** Rather, look for the lesson in it; ask the "why," make a plan—and move forward.

With a resilient mindset you are interested in learning and growing. You love challenges. You think ahead, calculating possible answers. When the outcome is a success, you confidently choose your next challenge. Your challenges are often demanding. When we attain success, we know the hard work was worth it! Bingo! If you have not been successful, ask yourself why. Regroup! Determine what your next action must be. Ensure that you have been using the exercises properly and frequently. *Revisit each exercise as if it is the first time you are doing it.*

Self-motivation: have a goal, a desire, and a plan to achieve! Believe in yourself, in your ability to develop and grow from steady effort. Be responsible. Resolve to be successful. You are aware of the difficulties ahead. You choose to overcome them and enjoy the challenge.

Having a resilient mindset you understand you can alter many situations to make them more palatable. On occasion, you choose to study something purely because it is not your best subject. You enjoy the challenge. You delight in assessing your progress, knowing where you are and visualizing **The Goal Within Reach.** This "take charge" approach puts you into the driver's seat. You have a keen sense of who you are, what you want and the effort needed to get there. In this case, you seek to overcome the anxiety you experience at exam time. Through personal effort and support you make it happen.

Revisit your exercises; do them again!

Learning is your interest and sitting exams anxiety free is one of your goals.

By taking this approach, you monitor your state when you take exams. If you studied the subject, with the required hours and dedication to learning, and applied the appropriate, suggested exercises for exam anxiety control, *your confidence levels at exam time will be excellent.* However, if the exam results were disappointing, of course you will be disappointed. Learn from the experience, and you will be able to assess weaknesses in your responses to questions asked.

Take charge and find out what you could have done differently. Is even more effort required, or is a new study method needed? Make the changes. You find this a welcome challenge and take full responsibility for the change. In fact, you love the challenge. You now understand any set-back can be a learning experience. You will do better next time. You feel in charge. Consider taking an exam as a way to prove to yourself that you know the material. Ask the teacher, etc. for examples of earlier exams to study. Show the teacher you intend to ace the next paper. Have enjoyment in the journey, while you are at it.

Remember: an exam cannot show you how smart you are, nor measure your potential. An exam is a snapshot in time and nothing more. Relax and focus, dig deep to find out what you know and use the results of your exam as feedback to grow. **Oh, Yes—Revisit the Exercises again!!**

A "growth mindset" means taking action and making an effort to reduce exam anxiety. Already, you have been introduced to Brain Gym® and Emotional Freedom Techniques to reduce anxieties as they arise.

Make regular practice of them.

You have been introduced to the importance of developing a "growth mindset."

[1] Dweck, Carol, Ph.D. *Mindset: The New Psychology of Success.* New York, Random House. 2006. P. 6.

[2] Dweck, Carol, Ph.D. *Mindset: The New Psychology of Success.* New York, Random House. 2006. P. 6

[3] Dweck, Carol, Ph.D. *Mindset: The New Psychology of Success.* New York, Random House. 2006. P. 7

CHAPTER 8
Goal Setting

What Is Goal Setting?

Goal setting is a method used to decide what is to be accomplished, plus a plan on how to achieve the desired results. Creating goals indicates you understand what you want in life, and further, that you are willing to take the steps necessary to achieve them.

Goal setting helps you to consider goals that may appear extremely difficult to achieve, but possible. If your mindset at the outset indicates the goal is unattainable this will haunt your every effort. However, if you consider the task difficult, but possible, that is quite another story. Careful examination of a difficult task may show that by breaking the overall, large job into smaller, manageable segments, success may be achieved.

Tracking success enroute to your goals is important. It gives you added focus to the journey. Examining your progress is also wonderful encouragement. When you notice the subject studied seems to be less of a struggle, it promotes even greater effort in your studies. Thoughts of procrastination become fewer as you advance toward your goal. Confidence increases with the continued use of the exercises; thoughts of exam anxiety diminish. An additional tool to encourage structured study is the use of a notebook to set down the following:

1. Date of study.
2. The subject studied.
3. The time use in the study.
4. Notes on comprehension, or difficulty with same. Page number, etc. Important.
5. State revisiting the "difficult" pages. Comments on re-reading.
6. Have you asked for assistance from the teacher re: difficult passages? (Any encouragement? Any support? There are answers out there!).

Let's do the Brain Gym® and EFT exercises again, right from the beginning!

One of the benefits of achieving success, through goal setting is the self-confidence it develops. When you are successful, applaud yourself, and those who supported you. You learn from your experience. Do what works. Avoid what does not. If unsuccessful, you hold yourself wholly accountable or responsible. This spurs you on to a renewed, more vigorous effort.

Another benefit of goal setting—it is personal and meaningful. You are more likely to be motivated and happy on your road to success. Many smaller goals reached makes the goal seem all the more achievable. Yes!

Steps to Goal Setting

1. Use an effective Goal Setting Structure:
The structure of the SMART goal helps you state your goal very clearly, completely. By so doing, you expand the possibility of achieving success.

Here is what SMART represents:
S = Specific
M = Measurable
A = Active
R = Realistic
T = Timed

Using the SMART structure could appear as follows.

I will achieve calm confidence (meaning being focused, eager, physically relaxed, breathing deeply, recalling information easily, etc.) during *all my* exams or during my *name a subject e.g. Physics* exams. I will measure my progress by using a scale of 0 – 10 and record in writing how I felt during my exams between now and January 1. I will use Brain Gym® and EFT to disperse the butterflies should they arise. I will develop a growth mindset, learn and practice the study skills, learning methods and practice self-care. I resolve to achieve this goal. I am capable of learning and using my knowledge, and skills to accomplish my goal by *set a specific date; e.g. January 1, 20--.*

You can see the above goal follows the SMART structure:

S= Specific - *of calm confidence – meaning focused, eager, physically relaxed, breathing deeply, able to recall information easily during (all my) or (Physics) exams*
M= Measurable – *using a scale of 0 – 10 and recording how I felt writing exams between now and January 1, 20—*
A= Active – *will use Brain Gym® and EFT to calm the butterflies, develop a   growth mindset, learn and practice the study and exam-taking skills, use the learning methods and practice self-care*
R= Realistic – *It is realistic for me to learn and use the above knowledge, skills and practices to accomplish my goal*
T= Timed – *January 1, 20--*

2. Write Down Your Goals, Review Them Daily, and Share Them

Research shows that when you write down your goals to paper we have a greater chance of achieving them.[1] Other research indicates that doing a daily review of our goals with a significant person in our life, we have a greater chance of achieving those goals. Review with someone who has a genuine interest in your life, in your success. Mothers, fathers, husbands, wives, tutors would be in this category.

Start by writing down your SMART goal for overcoming exam anxiety, review it daily with someone who has your best interest at heart. Compound the Brain Gym® and EFT exercises in your mind. Know them as well as you know your own name – and your goal!

3. Understand the Power of Goal Setting

Goal setting is very powerful and rewarding. It can help you decide what is important in your life. It can help you decide what actions to take, and when. It will also determine what to avoid. For example: consider yourself training to be an archer, but the best archer you can possibly be. Your goal is to be able to hit the bulls-eye with the arrow every time. Initially, you will know you are not gifted like Robin Hood. Some arrows will not make it to the target stand, never mind the bulls-eye.

To achieve such skill, consider the practice, persistence, knowledge, concentration and focus you must devote to the task. The archer too, had a goal. He wished to be a fine archer. Many hours over long periods of time were required to perfect his skill. In a similar way when you set your goal – let's say to dispel exam anxiety – persistence, concentration etc. are your requirements. Go and do it! You know the exercises, the tools to make you skilled at negating exam anxiety.

Concentration and focus are needed to hit that target. Consider the knowledge and skills, the practice and persistence you need. Now, relate this to your goal, or target, to achieve calm confidence at exam time. Your goal requires not only knowing specifically what you want to achieve, but also the focus and concentration knowledge and skills, practice and persistence to get there. It means that you will be able to identify and remove distractions that could side-track you from your goal.

Consider a great violinist in front of an orchestra. How did she achieve that skill on the violin? Along with talent, it was practice, practice, practice. All the talent in the world would not cut it if there were not constant practice. We, too, in our field of interest, must practice our exercises diligently, to both control exam anxiety and reach our goals.

Another metaphor to use is that of being in a sailboat. If you have no idea of a destination and no hand on the tiller, your sailboat will float aimlessly on the water, buffeted by the wind in one direction, and the waves in another. You will end up somewhere. However, if you have a map, a compass, and a destination you wish to reach, you will set the sails (knowledge and skills) and manage the rudder (focus, concentration, practice and persistence) and tack toward your destination using your compass. The wind can buffet the boat, waves can toss her around, but as long as your focus is on your destination, and you are managing the sails and rudder, you will arrive at your desired port. Your port is anxiety-free exams. Ok, skipper, you take the helm!!!!

Consider how this can relate to your daily life. With focus, you can override things that distract, and tempt you away from what you need to do to achieve your goal. These distractions can be tempting. Remember, when you are working towards a goal, you WILL be learning new things. This takes effort, focus, and complete involvement. Keeping your goals foremost in your mind is an ongoing, daily task.

4. Long-Term vs. Short-Term Goals

Depending what they are, *long-term goals* are those things that take a year or longer to achieve. In your case, one of your goals may be graduation from high school, college or university. Yet another may be to secure a scholarship which may entail two or more years of community involvement as well as a required grade-point average.

Just thinking about long-term goals can be daunting. That is why it is important to have a solid, workable strategy. So, write down your end goal and you will achieve it. THINK POSITIVELY! Remember the archer and say "I will hit that bulls-eye if it's the last thing I do!"

Then, work backwards, thinking out what goals you will need to achieve each year, each month and each week to get there. Write them down as SMART goals. Include them in your calendar, share them with a significant person in your life and review them daily. Here you will need to prioritize and decide what actions require attention first, second, third, and so on.
At the end of each week, assess how you are progressing and make adjustments along the way. Be brutally honest about your

progress. Like the sailor—make adjustments as you go. Be flexible and modify your study habits as you develop and learn. Short-term goals are those goals you wish to achieve within a year or less; perhaps completing a year of high school, college or university with a specified grade-point average; completing a requirement for a scholarship, and, of course, overcoming exam anxiety. Others may simply be goals which are not related to your larger, long-range goals like running a certain distance within an allotted time. For each of these short-term goals, there will be smaller goals. Set each up as a SMART goal to measure your progress towards your end goal.

5. Believe You Can

Henry Ford said, *"Whether you think you can or you think you can't, you're absolutely right."* Your belief impacts your chance of achievement. It is important to monitor your self-talk and your beliefs. Be aware that self-doubt and fear are normal. Anything that stretches you beyond your comfort zone, can definitely be nerve wracking. Nelson Mandela said, *"I learned that courage was not the absence of fear, but the triumph over it. The brave man is not he who does not feel afraid, but he who conquers that fear."*

Fear is one method your subconscious mind uses to protect you. Listen to it. Find out what you need to do to quieten the fears. Fear of the unknown can be allayed if we confront it. Would it help to reduce fear if you asked questions about a course, etc.? Is the worry unjustified? Wait a moment; let's regroup and do some Brain Gym® activities; use EFT; and review your goals until your self-confidence is regained! Where the fear is still justified in your mind, could the Gold Standard EFT and working with a certified EFT practitioner help?

When practice is not enough, contact a certified Brain Gym® consultant/practitioner for more in-depth practice of Brain Gym® and/or a certified EFT practitioner of Gold Standard EFT.

6. Keep an Open Mind

As you work towards your goals, be aware of opportunities that may arise. You might be given information, skills, make personal connections, or enjoy an experience that sets you up for even greater success.

7. Competence = Confidence and Higher Self-Esteem

As you set and achieve goals, not only do you develop competence, but also confidence and self-esteem. Believe in yourself and your ability to overcome challenges e.g. exam anxiety, that you face in life. Let's do some Brain Gym® and EFT while we are thinking about it.

[1] http://www.dominican.edu/dominicannews/study-highlights-strategies-for-achieving-goals

CHAPTER 9
Study Habits, Learning Methods and Exam-Taking Skills

Study habits, learning methods, and exam-taking skills are covered in this chapter. When you have a "growth mindset," you are always open to learning; developing new skills; growing in understanding; and expanding your horizons. This is your opportunity to do just that. There is much already written on these topics which you can get from books and websites on the internet.

Let's distinguish between study habits and learning methods. Studying means focusing on learning; Rudyard Kipling wrote the following words:

I keep six honest serving men.
They taught me all I know.
*Their names were **What** and **Why** and **When**.*
*And **How** and **Where** and **Who**.*

Most of us have been told to study, and learn. Seldom, however, are we taught how to do either one effectively. As you read through this chapter, check off what you already know and do.

Identify and start to use those things which are new. We repeat: **the more you practice and use these tools, these skills, the easier they will become — with more positive results.**

For those things you do to focus on the actual learning itself, we use "learning methods." Included in the learning method is *mind mapping*. Research, has found it to be a most effective learning tool.

Identify and start to use those methods which may be new to you. Keep in mind, the more you practice and use these habits, and skills, the easier they will be to use. Reflect on how your use of them has reduced your *exam anxiety* and improved exam results. **Persist! Practice!** Any skills and discipline you develop with these instructions will always be your strength.

Study Habits to Reduce Exam Anxiety

Studying is essential for everyone who not only wishes to excel but who also wishes to reduce exam anxiety. In her research, Dr. Dweck found that some students had the belief that only students who were not smart needed to study. Such a belief is absolutely folly. Students of every ability benefit from studying.

Perhaps you need to improve in all or many of your study habits. How is your organization, goal setting, attitude, and time management? How are your reading and writing skills? How are your skills at exam time? You will learn about these in the next section.

As mentioned earlier, the brain develops and grows when we challenge ourselves to learn new things. Students developing disciplined study and application change the brain to support such behavior. This will help them to succeed in any endeavor where there is genuine interest.

Here are some important study habits.

Six Study Habits for Successful Learning

1. Study Area to Support Your Learning
Choose a study area where you can work without distraction. Work in a well-lit room at a desk with a light which is on the opposite side of your dominant hand. Sit in a sturdy chair—one that will support good posture for optimum energy and mental clarity. Keep the room temperature cool so that you remain alert. Be proactive.

To avoid the temptation of computer games, or phone calls. Make cell phones off limits! Arrange that these are out of reach during your study time, preferably in another room. You can chat on the phone and play games AFTER YOU ACE YOUR

EXAM, ANXIETY free! You might want to consider using them as a reward once you have accomplished part, or all of your studies.

You may want to put a **"Do not disturb"** sign on your door. If they understand English, they should stay away. Period! Friends will do as you request. When you have set a study schedule for yourself, let your family and friends know the days and times when you are off limits.

Avoid studying on your bed or in front of the TV. What was showing on the TV will not be a question at exam time. You may find that you study best in short spurts. There are those that recommend that you have a timer set for twenty minutes. When it rings, stand up, stretch, walk around a few steps and take a sip of water and return to study. After an hour of studying perhaps do some Brain Gym® and then back to study. Do what works best for you. There are no absolutes in studying; our goal is learning!!!

Your study space is best free of clutter!! Have any materials you need for study close at hand. Have your pens, pencils, books, notebooks, calculator, rulers, protractors, calendar, dictionary, and water placed conveniently so that you can access them easily.

If you learn best visually, incorporate visual aids. The same is true if you are an auditory learner, include listening as part of your study practice. If kinesthetic, involve tactile strategies (for examples go to http://www.kinestheticlearningstrategies.com/) and whole body movement. *Include what you need for **optimum** learning.*

Remember: have water to sip throughout your study time.

2. Set Realistic Goals for Yourself.
This is important. Draw up your plan before the school year begins. Write down your SMART long-term and short-term goals. Write them down, share them with a significant person in your life and review them daily. In her research, Dr. Gail Matthews, professor in the Dominican University of California's Department of Psychology, found that more than seventy percent of her research subjects who not only wrote down their goals but also shared their goals with a friend or colleague were successful in achieving them. Compared to thirty-five percent who kept their goals to themselves and did not write them down.[1] You be one of the 75% mentioned by Dr. Matthews.

Write your goals down. Share them with someone who is a good listener and a confidante. It is important to keep them in one place. Hold to those goals and review them daily. **Read and repeat them out loud.** Visualize achieving them and how that will make you feel. YES! These strategies combined will be very helpful in boosting your motivation, confidence and determination.

What would you like to be? An Engineer, Doctor, Architect, Artist, Musician, Social Activist? Choose a career goal, as one of your SMART long-term goals. This can motivate you knowing that what you are doing in school is meaningful to you. If you are unsure what it is, write down your best guess. This goal will be related to your studies. Be open to the possibility that this goal may be modified as you develop in knowledge. Change is constant in life. You learn new things, develop new interests, and change in circumstances as opportunities arise. Be ready for such changes. All learning has value. You will seldom regret learning something in one field and then moving to some other field of endeavor.

Now that your SMART long-term goals have been written down, write down your short-term SMART goals. The more specific you are, the more effective your goals will be. These short-term goals can include your study schedule; the marks you will work to achieve in each of your subjects; what you will do to achieve them; your attitude and daily habits. Attending school, your extra-curricular activities, etc. should be on that list, too. Have a good-sized notebook where you record your SMART long-term and short-term goals. Number the pages and have a table of contents with page numbers. Remember, you are an organized student! When you have achieved the goals be sure to celebrate, and then write "Achieved" on your list.

As well as academic goals, set goals for other aspects of your life, too. Consider your social, physical, environmental, intellectual and spiritual goals. Do your best to create a well-rounded life while studying by setting SMART goals for these other aspects of your life, too. JUST REMEMBER, YOUR GOALS ARE NOT A BOAT BLOWN AROUND IN THE WIND.

3. Attend all Classes and Take Notes
Attending class is essential to your success. Classes are where you get the course outline, handouts, and the lab information. Class is where you engage in active note taking; receive hints from the teacher on what is important for you to know and study for exam time.

See below a summary of the *Concise Learning Method*[2] and where note-taking is discussed. This method of learning can be very effective. It engages the whole brain, and mirrors the way the cells in our brains connect. Thus, it can help you understand concepts; grasp the big picture; remember important details; and be fully engaged in the learning process by interacting with the information in a meaningful way.

4. Take Your Notes by Hand Using Cursive Writing
Carla Hannaford discusses how learning, understanding, retaining information and self-expression are connected to cursive writing. Please see Appendix I for her explanation of why using cursive writing is beneficial for brainstorming, mind-mapping, essay and exam writing. See how a beautifully written test using cursive can influence the person marking the test, too.

5. Have the Right Mental Attitude
Attitude is key to your study success and the "growth mindset" section above covers this aspect of studying. "I am a winner because I choose to be. I act and think like a winner."

6. Be Well Organized: Organize Supplies; Manage Time
Organization is a skill that may be learned and developed. You will never regret being organized, no matter your position in life. Organization will save you time. It will reduce stress when you find yourself with a deadline. Being organized and clutter-free can influence how you feel about the space in which you work. It will echo your uncluttered mind, your clarity of focus.

Have separate binders for each class. Own a three-hole punch — many handouts don't have holes. Date each handout. Place the most recent handout on top of earlier handouts. Have file folders in hanging files in a milk crate or file cabinet. Arrange them alphabetically and mark them clearly for easy access.

Have a calendar where you record your daily schedule; from wake-up in the morning to bedtime. Include school time and study time. Include a **daily review time** of what you learned in each class. Include weekly reviews where you spend an afternoon or evening reviewing what you have learned that week. Finally, include **in-class reviews** that take place over a few days prior to exams. Include in your notes all that might be on the exam. (Be sure to do this for each subject.) This is where your organization skills pay big dividends. Everything in its place. That's the winner's method!

Include on your calendar part-time jobs or volunteer work. You need to remember other items. It could be the deadline for a project; submitting an application; it could be an interview; a doctor's appointment, and mid-term and end-of-year exams. How about holidays and people's birthdays? Schedule in exercise and relaxation times. Schedule library times. Follow the schedule and adjust it to be most effective for you. Learning and growing, you will always be busy. However, you will be doing what you believe is in your best interest. It is your life! As Shakespeare wrote: "to thine own self be true."

A weekly schedule could look something like this. You fill in the detail …

Time	Mon	Tues	Wed	Thurs	Fri	Sat	Sun
7:00	Breakfast						
8:00	Travel / Possible study time						
9:00							
10:00							
11:00							
12:00	Lunch						
1:00							
2:00							
3:00						Set aside some study time on Saturday	
4:00							
5:00	Travel / Possible study time						
6:00	Dinner						
7:00					Take a break on Friday if you can. Reward yourself for all your hard work during the week.		
7:30	Study Subject #1 /2						
8:00						Same study schedule followed Mon - Thurs	
8:30	Study Subject #3/4						
9:00							
9:30	Study Subject #5 &						
10:00							
10:30	Recreation/Relaxation						
11:00	Sleep						

Prepare for the next day before going to bed. Fill your water bottle, make your lunch and set out your clothes. Have your books and notebooks packed, ready to go. Before going to sleep make a to-do list for the next day so you are prepared. The subconscious will work on this during your sleep for the best outcome. Place your alarm clock somewhere in your room where you need to get up in order to turn it off. That way, you force yourself to get up out of bed with less chance of sleeping in. Set your alarm at a time so that you do not need to rush to school. Ensure you have enough time to dress and eat a hearty breakfast. Arrange to get to school fifteen minutes before the first class begins. That way you can get settled; perhaps take some time to do a little Brain Gym® and prepare for learning. Again, practice makes perfect. The more you get into the habit of doing this, the easier it can become.

If you are challenged with being organized, consider working with a Brain Gym® practitioner. It is possible to anchor good organizational skills into your body/brain system for greater results.

7. Exam Preparation Skills
The best ways to reduce exam taking anxiety is to be well prepared. You have read above how to do away with cramming. Make review a continuous exercise all semester. Include this review as part of your daily study schedule. This will be natural

when you use the *Concise Learning Method* discussed below. Remember to use Brain Gym® and EFT to maintain a positive confident attitude. Getting some physical exercise before an exam will help reduce stress, too. Enjoying a good night's sleep before the exam is very important.

Budget your time. Ensure you have sufficient time to study for the exam. Go to any reviews that are available. Pay attention to hints that the teacher may give about the exam. Take careful notes. Ask questions about items that still confuse. Make sure you go to the class right before the exam—the teacher may give hints on the exam format. Go over any material you have from previous exams; from review material; previous homework; sample problems; the textbook, class notes. All these might indicate what the teacher thought were most important in the course.

Here now is an effective learning method.

The Concise Learning Method (CLM) for Effective Learning and Confidence Building

How would you like an effective method that can help you learn; understand at a deep level; and remember information from each of your classes plus aid to overcome exam anxiety? How would you like to know a method that can help you to manage information from each of your classes without feeling overwhelmed? How would you like to a skill for writing essays on any subject, and prepare you effectively for writing exams? The *Concise Learning Method* created by Toni Krasnic is that method. In this section I will summarize and give the key benefits of this method and why it can be so effective. However, to learn how to use it, I suggest you get his books, ***How to Study with Mind Maps; The Concise Learning Method and Mind Mapping for Kids,*** and visit his website www.conciselearning.com.[3] You might want to know that the CLM is based on solid principles of learning psychology and students have found it to be a most helpful learning tool.

In the *Concise Learning Method* you develop mind maps in five stages (Prepare, Participate, Process, Practice and Produce) in order to learn. During each stage you create your mind maps, ask key questions; analyze the information; understand, draw conclusions, see connections, and develop deeper, newer understandings. During each of these stages you will find it easier to remember information using the mind maps because you have been constructing the connections based on your understanding of the material. This is due to the active, engaged role you employed in their creation.

Below is an example of a simple mind map. You identify a key concept, then topic and sub-topics. To help further remember the information on the mind map, you can differentiate concepts by using a multitude of colors, add graphics and pictures.

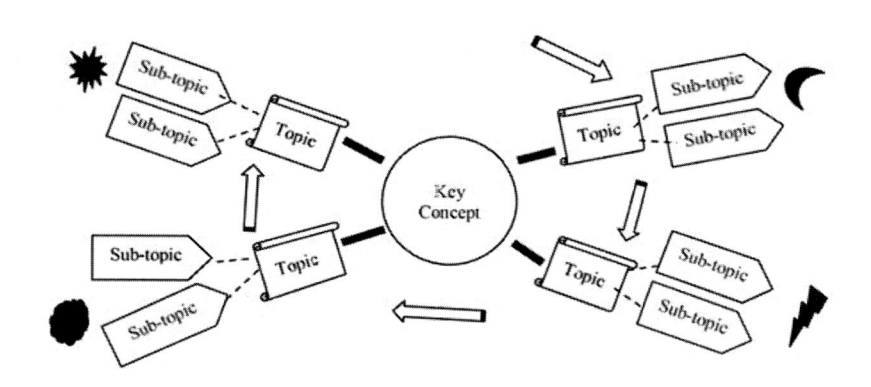

The mind mapping format mimics in part the way the brain functions—that is by neurological connections. That is one of the reasons it is so effective. Yet another reason it is considered to be so effective is it engages *both sides of your brain:* the visual, creative and big-picture orientation of the **right brain hemisphere** and the logical and detail orientation of the **left brain hemisphere.**

When you use the ***CLM*** to study from a textbook, Krasnic suggests that you take the chapter that your teacher is focused on at the time; that you write the **key concept** of the chapter in the middle of the page. In this case, the key concept will be the chapter title. **The topics** will be the bolded headings you find within the chapter. And the sub-topics will be those bold-type items that follow each topic. At this stage, there is no need to get any more detailed. **This is the preparation stage.**

Once you have set out the concepts of the chapter in this way, take your mind map with you to class, and add information you learn from the teacher to the appropriate locations on your map. This is the **participation** stage. Unlike being a passive recipient of information in the rote note-taking method, here you are engaged and participating in what you are learning. You are applying the information to the different topics, asking questions for clarification, and actively acquiring both the big picture and details on the subject.

In the **processing stage**, that is the third stage of mind mapping, you study the chapter in greater detail, and add more information. Additional information gathered from other sources can be added. You are engaged, are active in your understanding each step of the way.

The next stage is the **practice stage**. Now apply what you have learned. Here you find out what you understand, how to apply it and what gaps may need attention.

The last is the **production stage** in the form of presentations, writing papers or exams.

Mind mapping is also highly effective because many of the following memory techniques[4] used to help you remember information are, or can be, incorporated into it. Consider the following:

1. **Chunking**

   It is easier to memorize information when you break it up into small chunks. This is exactly what is done in mind mapping.

2. **Understanding**

   Before you begin trying to memorize something understand it first. Mind mapping is a process of developing and connecting ideas for deeper understanding.

3. **Graphic organizers**

   Mind mapping is a form of graphic organizing. These graphic organizers (knowledge maps, web maps, tree diagrams, structure diagrams, web diagrams, etc.) can take different forms depending on the task at hand.

4. **Visualization**

   Visualization can help you remember things very well. The web design itself is visual as are the colors and graphics that you can add to it for greater effect.

5. **Association**

   Mind mapping is all about making connections both with the information that you are learning and also with your own previous experience and understanding.

6. **Other methods** to help you remember include rhyming, storytelling, talking, writing sentences, creating acronyms, rehearsing, and playing games. Any of these can be part of your process in the mind mapping method.

Mind mapping is a tremendously effective learning tool and an answer to all those who are looking for ways to learn effectively, and meaningfully. It is a great complement to the "growth mindset" discussed above, a perfect fit with Brain Gym® and the Dominance Factor. It is a great tool to develop confidence to replace anxiety on exam day.

Fran Burke, M.Ed.

Exam-Taking Tips: Tips for the Night before an Exam; General To-Do Tips; Multiple Choice, Essay, Short Answer Tips

1. The Night before and Day of the Exam

- During the weeks and days leading up to your exam, you have been reviewing and doing your best to understand the material that will be on your exam. Your exam is taking place the next day and you want to be at your best.
- Start by having a good nutritious dinner around five or six p.m. the night before.
- Avoid reviewing for the rest of the evening if you possibly can. Relax, and take your mind off the next day's exam. You could include some Brain Gym® and Tapping during this time.
- You may want to avoid any caffeinated beverages and looking at a computer screen or TV one to two hours before going to bed. (The light from these electronic devices can interfere with the ability to fall asleep.)
- Before going to bed prepare everything you need to take with you to the exam. Have the pens, pencils (sharpeners or extra lead), erasers, rulers, protractors, calculators, batteries, textbooks to return, house keys, transit fare, etc. organized in your book bag, ready to confidently grab and go.
- Take a watch with you so you can time yourself.

- Be sure to fill your water bottle; have it in your bag, too. You will want to sip water during your exam to help keep your mind clear and focused.
- Plan to go to bed so that you get a good eight to ten hours of sleep.
- Set your alarm in a location where you have to get out of bed in order to shut it off. If you have the tendency to sleep through your morning alarm, set a back-up alarm, too.
- Set your alarm so that you have time to eat breakfast.
- Have the right kind of breakfast that will give you sustained energy and help you focus. (Avoid refined carbohydrates as you may experience a drop in blood sugar during your exam.)
- Plan to arrive at your exam location a minimum of fifteen minutes before the exam starts. Take traffic issues into consideration and plan for them.
- When you get to your destination, take some time to relax and do some Brain Gym® and Tapping. As mentioned above, this can integrate and help prepare your system for optimum confidence and calm. If students around you are anxious, get them to join you so you can spread your calm confidence to them. Avoid students who are spreading anxiety to others.
- Be sure to go to the bathroom before entering the exam room.

2. General To-Do Tips

- When you go into the exam room, choose a comfortable spot with plenty of room around you.
- When you sit down to your exam, take a sip of water, a few slow deep breaths and remind yourself that you are well-prepared and will do well.
- Get out your pens, pencils, calculators, etc. and put them on the desk in front of you.
- Maintain a good posture throughout the exam.
- Anytime you start to feel anxious calm yourself with positive thoughts, slow deep breaths, Brain Gym® and Tapping.
- Write your name clearly in the space allotted.
- Read the instructions slowly and carefully.
- Ask the teacher to explain instructions that are not clear to you.
- Preview the exam so that you have a good idea how it is structured, how many points are allotted to each question, how much time to review the exam before handing it in, and from that information, decide how much time to give to each section.
- Then, take some time to write down important information like definitions or formulas, in the margin to help relax your mind and retrieve information from your memory more easily.

- To build up your confidence for the harder questions, do the questions you know the answers to, first. (For harder questions that will take up more of your time, leave for last if you can do so without losing marks.) Your subconscious mind will be working on the harder questions while you are working on the easier ones.
- Do the questions that have the largest number of marks as soon as you have done the easiest ones first.
- Unless you are penalized for answering questions wrong, answer all questions.
- Be sure to write *clearly and with proper spelling, grammar and punctuation.* If the marker cannot read your writing or you express yourself poorly, chances are your answer will be marked wrong.
- Think about how your teacher would answer the question and from what viewpoint and answer accordingly.
- Know words and their definitions and be able to apply them.
- Be familiar with exam terminology (see chart below).
- For difficult questions, underline the key words to help get clarification and rephrase the question to not change the meaning but to understand them more clearly.

EXAM TERMINOLOGY [7]

Analyze: Divide something into parts or steps and look at each part in detail. Then look at how the parts connect to one another.

Apply: Use your skill/knowledge in various ways.

Classify: Sort objects or ideas into groups according to their similarities.

Compare: Show the similarities and the differences between two or more things.

Contrast: Show only the differences between two or more things.

Criticize: Describe the positive and negative features of a subject then make a judgment about which features are most significant.

Define: Give a clear meaning that fits the situation.

Demonstrate: Show how you arrived at an answer.

Describe: Use words to give a detailed picture of something. Include all its important elements or features.

Design: In your mind, forma plan or an arrangement of detail for a project.

Develop: Work through a plan or an idea or a project step-by-step to reach a goal or clearly defined objective.

Discuss: Look in detail at all sides of a situation or an idea and make a judgment about which details are most significant and give your reasons.

Edit: Review your writing in draft form and make changes that strengthen word choices, sentences, and paragraphs.

Examine: Look into all parts of a subject in detail.

Explain: Tell the meaning of something in your own words. Tell why or how something means what it does or give reasons for something.

Evaluate: Analyze or discuss something and make a judgment on its importance, significance, usefulness, or worth.

Graphically Organize: Show facts or ideas in a chart, a graph, a map, a web a diagram. Include labels.

Identify: Tell what something is by describing its features or characteristics.

Illustrate: Give an example to make an explanation or idea understandable.

Interpret: Tell the meaning of something.

Investigate: Identify and resolve issues about which there are confusions or differences.

Justify: Give reasons, support, or proof when you make a judgment or choice.

Organize: Put ideas, facts, and opinions into an order that fits your purpose.

Outline: Arrange details of a subject under headings and subheadings.

Persuade: Give convincing details or reasons to support an idea or opinion.

Plan: Think out and arrange the details of your work beforehand.

How to End Exam Anxiety

Predict: Use knowledge of a situation to say what will come next.

Proofread: Go over writing in draft form to correct spelling and punctuation.

Prove: Use facts or reasons to show that something is true.

Relate to: Show how all parts are connected to one another.

Research: Use a variety of sources to discover facts and ideas about a subject.

Review: Go over something in detail then make a choice or judgment.

Select: Choose, according to instructions or guidelines.

State: Give the main points in a logical order.

Support: Give facts, examples, and quotations to back up an idea or an opinion.

Summarize: Give all the main facts or ideas in a shortened form. Leave out details and examples.

Fran Burke, M.Ed.

3. Multiple Choice Exam-Taking Tips[8]

- Find out whether or not you will be docked for marks if you answer a question wrong. If you will not be docked for wrong answers, do your best to answer all of the questions doing your best to make the right choices.
- Read through each question while covering up the answers. Do your best to answer the question from what you remember. Only then look at the answers. (This way, tricky questions will be less likely to throw you off.)
- Do all the questions like this and answer all those you know and can answer quickly, first.
- Avoid spending too much time over questions the answers of which you are unsure until you have answered all of the easier questions first. You can go back to more difficult questions later.
- Be sure to read all the choices listed before choosing your answer. Cross off answers you know to be incorrect.
- The choice with the most information is more than likely the correct answer.
- Positive choices are more likely to be true than negative ones.
- Since your first choice is usually correct, do not change your answers unless you are sure of the correction or unless you misread the question.

- Things to consider in "All of the above" and "None of the above" choice questions:
  If you know one of the statements is true, do not choose "None of the above."
  If you know one of the statements is false, do not choose "All of the above."
- If there are at least two correct statements in an "All of the above" questions, then "All of the above" is most likely the answer.
- Review your answers before handing in the exam.
- Celebrate.

4. Essay Exam-Taking Tips[9]

- Think and plan before you start to write your essay.
- Be aware of the terminology being used in the instructions, i.e. compare, contrast, explain, describe, etc. as per above list of exam terminology.
- Be sure to structure your essay with the content requested in the instructions.
- Mind map your ideas quickly.
- Be concise about your main idea and specific about the supporting details.
- State your main idea in the topic or first sentence of your introductory paragraph and follow it with your supporting ideas.

- Use the rest of your essay to discuss these ideas in more detail depending on what is required. End with a concluding paragraph that wraps up your argument clearly and succinctly.

5. Short answer questions[10]

As the name implies, short answer questions require relatively short answers. To gauge if the answer should be a few words or a paragraph, or two, see how many marks are allocated for the question. In that way you can help base the length of you answer on both the question and the possible number of marks.

Generally, short answer questions are designed to find out if you are able to do such things as define terms and show understanding of them by being able to apply your definition. Or, they may be designed to demonstrate that you know the similarities and differences of something, or identify and explain a concept or theory.

When you answer your short answer questions, be brief and to the point. Organize your answer so it is clear and relevant. Do avoid adding unnecessary information – you will use up precious time that could be used to complete other questions and, by doing so, you will not get extra marks.

Before you begin, read through all the questions. Figure out how much time you have for each question and keep track of time. Answer those questions that are easiest and for which you know the answer first. Be sure to identify those questions that have more than one part to them e.g. you may be asked to give a definition of something and then to give some examples. Then, return to the more challenging questions and answer them the best you can.

True/False Tests Tips[11]

True/false sections on tests are very common. They can be tricky. The following tips are general rules of thumb and can help you maximize your results.

To start:

- Before choosing an answer, carefully read through each question at least twice. Pay close attention to each word as one word can make the difference between the statement being true or false.
- Start by looking at the statement as true. Then, if any part of the statement is not true, then you know it is a false statement.
  - ♠ Remember that if any part of the statement is false, then the entire statement is false. Stated another way, just

because part of a statement is true does not necessarily make the entire statement true.

- Know that true/false tests generally tend to have more true statements than false ones. If you are not going to be penalized by answering a question incorrectly, you might want to choose an answer as true when you have to guess.

- Statements that tend to be true are those that:
  ♠ Include exception words like "generally, commonly, often/usually, most/mostly, some/sometimes, frequently, may/maybe, partially, many," etc. These exception words mean that the statement can be considered true or false depending on the circumstances. Usually these types of qualifiers lead to the answer being true.

- Statements that tend to be false are those that:
  ♠ Use words that express absolutes like "never/always, absolutely/totally, no one/none, the best/worst, each/every, everyone/all, only," etc. mean that the statement must be true all of the time. Usually these types of qualifiers lead to a false answer because there often are exceptions.
  ♠ However, a statement like, the sun always rises in the east and always sets in the west is absolute and true.

♠ Statements that are only partially true are in fact false.

♠ A true-false statement is more likely to be false the longer the statement. There is more chance that one part of the statement can be false and consequently make the whole statement false.

♠ Statements tend to be false when they include cause-effect words like the reason that, because, caused, resulted in, etc., unless the statement also includes an exception word like generally, partially, some, sometimes.

♠ If a statement expresses an extreme idea, it tends to be false.
Negative prefixes and words like non-, un-, not, none, etc. can be tricky. Be sure to understand them in the context of the statement.

♠ If there is a double negative, such as "not unhappy" that means happy. The meaning will be positive.

---

[1] http://www.dominican.edu/dominicannews/study-highlights-strategies-for-achieving-goals

[2] Krasnic, Toni. *How to Study with Mind Maps: The Concise Learning Method.* Concise Books Publishing. 2014

[3] www.conciselearning.com.

[4] http://psychology.about.com/od/memory/ss/ten-facts-about-memory.htm#step

[5] www.dictionary.reference.com/browse/achievement by Oxford

[6] http://students.acu.edu.au/administration_and_enrolment/examinations_and_results/examinations/examination_tips/answering_the_questions/exam_tips_for_short_answer_questions

[7] http://www.openpolytechnic.ac.nz/study-with-us/study-rsources-for-studentsexams/tips-for-answering-exam-questions/different-types-of-exam-questions

[8] http://www.openpolytechnic.ac.nz/study-with-us/study-rsources-for-studentsexams/tips-for-answering-exam-questions/different-types-of-exam-questions

[9] http://www.openpolytechnic.ac.nz/study-with-us/study-rsources-for-studentsexams/tips-for-answering-exam-questions/different-types-of-exam-questions

[10] http://carleton.ca/lss/wp-content/uploads/TOP10-ShortAnswerExams.pdf

CHAPTER 10
Self Care

Self-care is essential if one is to live a happy, productive life. Overcoming anxiety is a bonus at any stage of life. It is essential in our formative years that anxiety, and in particular exam anxiety, be brought to heel.

Students of any age require a well-rounded lifestyle if they hope to achieve any success in education. Poor nutrition (among other negatives) will be a detriment to learning.

Here are five areas of self-care that need to be considered if we wish to overcome exam anxiety. These are:

1) positive self-talk
2) having a strong social network
3) a good nutritious diet
4) exercise and
5) enough quality sleep

These are key elements of physical health and mental well-being. Enjoying both mental and physical health, we are better equipped to function at your optimum in all aspects of your life. We will, in theory, be more resilient, confident and more capable of performing under stress, including sitting exams.

Self-Talk

Your self-talk can make the difference between a resilient and happy life and an inflexible and unhappy one. Because you are interested in finding ways to overcome exam anxiety, you will want to become aware of your self-talk because the more positive your self-talk the better will be your chances of succeeding. According to the Mayo Clinic

Self-talk is the endless stream of unspoken thoughts that run through your head. These automatic thoughts can be positive or negative. Some of your self-talk comes from logic and reason. Other self-talk may arise from misconceptions that you create because of lack of information. [1]

Self-talk can affect your self-confidence and self-esteem, and much more. Consider your health; well-being; outlook on life; attitude towards yourself; ability to make friends and feeling that you have some control over events in your life. That would be positive self-talk. Self-talk is known to reduce the incidence of depression, assists us to cope with hardships, produces feelings of well-being and possibly longer life. Positive self-talkers tend to exercise more, enjoy a healthier diet and refrain from alcohol and tobacco use.

Consider the effects of negative self-talk. If the thoughts are mostly negative, our outlook on life is likely pessimistic—"the glass as half-empty rather than as half-full." We are unable to look for "the silver lining." You may be hard on yourself when things go awry, or anticipate the worst. You may not look for the positive, hear or accept a compliment. You may not accept yourself unless you are absolutely perfect. This negative perspective, way of talking to yourself creates stress, a feeling of being a victim. It can take a toll on your health and sense of well-being. **IT IS UNHEALTHY!**

It is important that you develop an awareness of your self-talk. Because it can flow from the subconscious mind, it may be low level, and subtle. Listen to your thoughts. Be aware . . . ! Are they positive, or negative?

If negative, make the effort to change to positive self-talk. It takes practice, commitment and persistence because you are changing one habit for another. You are growing new neurological pathways. Each day, pay particular attention to your self-talk. When you have a thought that you would like to convert to positive, take a moment to write it down. Next to the negative thought, write down a positive statement to replace it. The positive statement needs to be something that you believe. For example:

Negative	Positive
I'll never do well on exams.	I am choosing to learn new strategies and this gives me hope that I will do better.
I'll never do well on exams.	If others can do it, so can I.
I'll never get into the university program I need for my future career. My life will be a failure.	I choose to do my best to achieve my goal and have a back-up plan that is a second best choice. I have a bright future ahead.
I'll never be perfect!	I choose to be satisfied with the marks I get and even if they are not perfect, they are close enough.
I'm such a loser and will never succeed.	I have succeeded before and, with effort and help, I choose to succeed again. If it is going to be, it is up to me. I choose to see myself as a winner.

Then, incorporate some Tapping with your statements. For example:

- *Even though **I catch myself thinking that I'll never do well on exams**, I deeply and completely love and accept myself.* Tap several rounds using this statement and reminder phrase.
- *After* you have tapped this through several times, have brought down the SUDS level and have taken a deep breath after each round, consider tapping in the positive.

*Even though **I catch myself thinking that I'll never do well on exams**, I am choosing to learn new strategies and this gives me hope that I will do better.*

- Tap several rounds using this statement and reminder phrase, remembering to take a deep breath after each round.
- **NOTE**: You can change up the wording to better reflect your thinking.
- **REMEMBER**: You need to acknowledge and accept what is before it can be replaced with something else. You have to remove the clouds before the sun can shine.

As you monitor your self-talk, be good to yourself. Congratulate yourself for even the smallest success. Take time to laugh. For fun, stand in front of a mirror and tell yourself positive things. Say them out loud. Remember that neurons that fire together, wire together. This means the more you do of this, the easier it is to do and the more it becomes a habit to support your success.

Strong Social Support[2]

Another aspect of self-care, is **having a social network** to provide: 1) a sense of security; 2) a sense of belonging and a way to stave off loneliness; and 3) a sense of self-worth by being called a friend. These are all important as you struggle with exam anxiety. You want to know that your social supports are there to encourage you when you are "down," and a safety-net when needed.

You rely on them to be there for you when needed, just as you would be there for them, should they need you. These all add ways to reduce the stress in your life.

Your social network will be those family members and friends who believe in you and want you to succeed. People who are positive, demonstrate resilience and optimism. They know what it is to struggle, to overcome barriers to success, they can be your cheerleaders, offer guidance and advice. They may possibly connect you to helpful resources when, or if needed.

If you need to develop this social support network, consider getting involved with people who share similar hobbies. Look for Meet-Ups in your area. Join a fitness club. Volunteer for something you feel passionate about. When you meet people with similar interests, call them, go out for coffee and keep in touch. Be a good listener, with lots of give and take.

Again, be sure to socialize with people who will help reduce the stresses in your life. These will be folks who are positive, have a healthy lifestyle, and are supportive. Assess people you are considering to be part of your social network. Do you feel energized when you are around them? If yes, then these are the people with whom you want to nurture relationships. AVOID NEGATIVE PEOPLE AT ALL COSTS!

How to End Exam Anxiety

Here is a quote from the Mayo Clinic that you will want to keep in mind;

Taking the time to build a social support network is a wise investment not only in your mental well-being but also in your physical health and longevity. Research shows that those who enjoy high levels of social support stay healthier and live longer. So don't wait.[2]

Another way to get support is to find a mentor, i.e. someone who has already been a student, and who, perhaps overcame the difficulties of exam anxiety or other forms of anxiety. If you have exam anxiety in only one or two subjects, you might want to chat with someone who is knowledgeable in those subject areas. Such a person can offer invaluable tips that you can use to help you overcome your challenge. Keep in mind—a mentor is not someone whom you pay, as you would a consultant or an advisor. A mentor is someone who is interested in your success and is, no doubt, pleased that you would choose them for advice.

Who might you go to as a sounding board? How about choosing someone on LinkedIn, your Community Centre, Meet-ups or Facebook? Be alert for discussions about exam anxiety—or performance anxiety. When you find someone whom you think could be helpful to you, check and make sure the person is safe. Then ask if they would have some time to talk. Know precisely what you would like to discuss. You will want to tell them about yourself and exam anxiety. Relate your difficulties and what you have done to overcome them, and what did or didn't work.

When you have managed to conquer your own challenges through the support of a mentor, consider becoming a mentor, too. Be a cheerleader for someone else.

Nutrition

Taking care of your physical health is important for success. You will provide sustained energy, a good clear mind and an overall sense of well-being in school. Be wise, be wary.

Eat only what is good for you. Mother Nature prepared these in the healthiest of ways. Temptations may arise, e.g. cigarettes, and alcohol. Neither will help you with exam anxiety, nor assist with questions on the exam paper!

If you are concerned about your nutrition, consult a nutritionist who can assess your condition. If need be, they will suggest improvement in your food regimen.

Know that natural, unprocessed food provides the better nutrition. Organically grown foods are understood to be healthier, however they may be more expensive.

Some things to consider about good eating habits: [3]

1. Eat three square meals a day including a good breakfast. A breakfast that will give you sustainable energy at the start of the day can help you ward off the cravings for foods that are less than healthy. Three square meals a day can help you burn fat by maintaining a healthy metabolism. By doing so, you can help ward off those mood and/or energy swings that can sometimes come with low-blood sugar.

2. Include healthy forms of protein. These can be nuts, seeds, beans, dairy, soy, lean beef, poultry and fish. Protein is essential for strong muscles, good metabolism, and possibly help reduce the risk of heart disease. Choose those which your body accepts without allergic reaction and fit into your philosophical framework. If you go totally vegetarian be sure to check with a nutritionist.

3. Whole grains not only add a good source of fiber which you need each day but also important vitamins. Some other benefits of adding fiber to your diet is to help control blood cholesterol, help reduce the risk of such diseases as bowel cancer and heart disease.

4. Fresh vegetables and fruit. Because they are so naturally high in vitamins, minerals and fiber and low in calories, your

diet is best to include at least five servings of vegetables and fruits each day. Instead of a candy bar or a bag of potato chips as a mid-morning or afternoon snack, consider some fresh carrot or celery sticks with a small piece of protein or some fruit and plain yogurt.

5. Have water. In the Brain Gym® section of this book, you have already learned about the importance of sipping water throughout the day to keep your body well hydrated. It is good to carry a non-plastic water canteen with water you have filtered when possible. Besides ingesting unhealthy chemicals that leach into the water from plastic bottles, you will be keeping plastic bottles out of landfill and oceans. So much damage is being done to the land and sea as a result of the plastic from these bottles, alone. If you are not sure how much water to drink, consult with a nutritionist. A general rule of thumb that I grew up with was eight glasses of water daily. (Refer back to the section on water in the Brain Gym® section.)

There is always more to learn about diet: what we eat, but also the way we eat. You may wish to read more about nutrition and explore the Mediterranean diet, or the Ayurvedic diet, Ayurveda being the ancient medical system of India. These can add a whole other dimension to understanding the influence of nutrition and diet in your life.

Improving the way you eat and what you eat is a choice. You may find it challenging to replace poor dietary choices and eating habits with better ones. Take slow steps and keep your goal of health and well-being your sole purpose. As you take these steps, notice how much better you feel physically and emotionally and how much more energy you have with more nutritious food choices. It is these benefits that you notice that can help to motivate you to continue on your path to better nutrition and food choices.

Exercise

For years we were warned about the dangers of smoking. That vice has been largely removed in society. Now we have another health warning: **we sit too much**. It is a common failing! Lack of exercise can cause ill health effects. Exercise can help maintain health and well-being. It needs to become a part of our daily or weekly routine.

Exercise can help improve: 1) the quality of sleep; 2) self-esteem; 3) your mood; 4) healthy weight; 5) stress reduction; 6) endurance; and 7) energy. These are the very qualities of mind and body helpful in overcoming exam anxiety and improved exam performance. Be sure to check with your doctor before starting any exercise routine to make sure it is the right one for you.

Fran Burke, M.Ed.

Dr. Joseph Mercola (born 1954), an alternative medicine proponent, and an osteopathic physician, identifies four types of exercise to help maintain your health. It is important to keep challenging your body to greater heights as you get proficient at any particular level. [4]

Mercola suggests that your routine incorporate these four types of exercise:

Type	Examples	Benefits
Aerobic Exercise	Walking quickly, jogging, cycling,	Helps to elevate oxygen in your blood, increase your stamina, improve your immune system, strengthen your heart, increase endorphins or natural pain killers
Interval Training	Alternate short bursts of high-intensity exercise with gentle recovery periods	Helps to condition your heart by improving your cardiovascular fitness, increase fat-burning capabilities, optimal weight and level of fitness, in a shorter amount of time
Strength Training	Use weights to exhaust your muscles. To do that, use weights that are heavy enough that you can do a repetition a maximum of 12 times and yet light enough that you can repeat the 12 reps for a total of four rounds. After exhausting your muscles, give them a rest of at least two days. They need that amount of time to recover, repair and rebuild.	For strength of muscles and bones.
Core Exercises:	Yoga and Pilates are exercise programs which help to strengthen your core muscles, the foundation for movement throughout your whole body.	Help protect and support your back, help make your body less prone to injury and help you gain greater balance and stability.

Exercising regularly is important for your health and well-being. The right amount of time for each type of exercise is for you to discover. There are fitness instructors, books, and websites to give you direction. If you interested, you may wish to look up Dr. Mercola on interval training (http://fitness.mercola.com/). He advocates it as a highly effective form of exercise.

Sleep

Are you getting enough sleep? Does it matter how long you sleep? Can the quality of sleep influence exam anxiety?

Anything that affects your health, your well-being, should be your concern. Many authorities on sleep advocate eight hours of sleep each night. This should be deep, sound sleep. If you are concerned about the quality of your sleep, see your family doctor. Lack of sleep can affect every aspect of learning, performance and health. How you feel during the day is a function of how well your body rested during the night. During sleep, your body is promoting healthy brain function and physical health.

Understand that getting enough sleep will make a difference in your ability to learn, concentrate and perform as in sitting in exams. Learning demands attention, concentration, memory, problem-solving, and creativity. All those elements are fostered by adequate sleep. Consider this: the happier you are with the minimum of mood swings, the easier it will be to learn and find joy in a more positive social life.

Noting the benefits of a good night's sleep you understand how important sleep is before an exam. Those all-nighters fail to provide the benefits of a good night's sleep. With that knowledge, you might do your last studying two days before an exam. The evening before the exam, relax. Get to bed and enjoy a deep restful sleep. Be in your optimum condition when you sit down at exam time.

How much sleep is enough? The Sleep Foundation[5] recommends the following hours of sleep per night as:

- School-age children (6-13): Sleep range 9-11 hours
- Teenagers (14-17): Sleep 8-10 hours
- Younger adults (18-25) and Adults (26-64): Sleep range is 7-9 hours

How many hours of sleep do you get at night? Are you getting the recommended sleep suggested above? Record how much sleep you get and note how you feel and function daily. Considering the recommended range above, do you do better on the smaller number of hours or the larger number of hours? How do you know?

- Are you alert during the day? Are you able to get by without caffeine?
- Are you able to control the amount you eat? Are you making nutritious choices most of the time? Are you keeping your weight down?
- Are you productive? Are you cheerful? Content?
- Do you sleep soundly and through the night?

If you answer yes to the questions above, you are doing well. If you need to make some improvements, what changes might you make?

Here are some basic guidelines to follow when it comes to sleep[6]. It is important to schedule your sleep as part of your daily routine and be disciplined in sticking to it. The habit of sleeping and waking at a regular time every day can aid you in getting the proper amount of sleep you need. Whenever possible, follow a routine that supports your sleep needs. In other words, include:

1) Having a regular sleep schedule seven days a week—even on weekends.
2) Making sure you have adequate exercise each day.
3) Knowing when to have your last caffeinated beverage (including soft drinks) during the day and then refrain from it after that time

4) Having a pillow and mattress that are comfortable.
5) Having a sleep area that is quiet and dark.
6) Having a sleep area that is neither too warm nor too cold.
7) Always having a relaxing routine before bedtime (a warm bath, meditation, muscle relaxation, gentle stretching, listening to calming music, a favorite hobby, reading from hard copy or listening to a book, newspaper, etc.).
8) Turning off all electronics (computers, TVs, cell phones, etc.) at least an hour before bedtime. They (a) can prevent the production of the sleep hormone, melatonin, that regulates your sleep/wake cycle; (b) interrupt your sleep due to the sounds they make; (c) keep your mind from being able to relax.
9) Leaving all electronics (including the TV) outside the room where you sleep.
10) Eating a little snack before sleep if it helps you to fall asleep, and include it in your routine.
11) Making a to-do list for the next day and setting it aside.
12) Keeping your bed a place only for sleeping so your mind associates it with this activity only.
13) Increasing your exposure to natural light.
14) Doing some Tapping.
15) Doing some Brain Gym® activities.

Conclusion

Self-care is essential for reducing exam anxiety. Positive self-talk, social support, proper nutrition, exercise and adequate sleep contribute to your overall health and well-being and are essential for doing and being at your best.

There is a lot to absorb throughout these pages. Consider how much of what is within them you would like to make a part of your life. Choose one or two that you think will help. Incorporate them into your day. Perhaps you could start by practicing one of the short-term strategies. Start with either the Brain Gym® activities or Tapping to reduce the immediate stress. Make one or both of them a part of your daily routine. While taking only a few minutes to do, their impact can be enormous in reducing your anxiety, and help you to function at your optimum level.

Then, scan through the long-term strategies and choose one or two that will be most helpful for you. Once included in your routine, choose another until you have transformed yourself from a person who is anxious at exam time to one who is eager to sit down and write an exam. That is the transformation I wish for you.

Fran Burke, M.Ed.

[1] http://www.mayoclinic.org/healthy-lifestyle/stress-management/in-depth/positive-th

[2] http://www.mayoclinic.org/healthy-lifestyle/stress-management/in-depth/social-support/art-20044445

[3] http://www.oxyfresh.com/news/ha_nutrition.asp

[4] http://fitness.mercola.com/

[5] http://www.helpguide.org/articles/sleep/how-to-sleep-better.htm

[6] http://www.helpguide.org/articles/sleep/how-to-sleep-better.htm

Appendix 1

OUR AMAZING HANDS: A CASE FOR CURSIVE
Carla Hannaford, Ph.D.

Our most important and complex bodily tools, taking a full 20 years to develop, are our hands. The trait that distinguishes primates and humans from other animals is our opposable thumb and the large motor and sensory cortex assigned to the hands. The importance of manipulation (hand movements) begins in utero, as fetuses suck their thumbs or fingers, continuing on in babies as they grasp with their hands and communicate through gesturing. Touch, movement and gestures are critical to learning.

The rich supply of nerve receptors that develop are not only essential for grasping, they are important for conscious perception. The touch receptors in our hands allow us to put our world together, to understand texture and structure that will formulate our reality. The more developed the hand, the more developed the brain.

Fran Burke, M.Ed.

As babies begin to move, the ear and hand move in tandem, assisting the baby to roll over, sit up and eventually crawl. The pressure on the hand during the act of crawling helps to build and stabilize the bony structure of the hand. As the baby begins to pull themselves up and eventually climb, the hands and upper arms are strengthened allowing the hands to become more mobile and exacting tools able to manipulate the environment. A more developed brain occurs with rich and varied hands-on exploration, helping children to learn and remember more. Children who had played with blocks the most had higher math scores in seventh grade. Encouraging a child to draw at an early age also assists writing and creativity later on. Children naturally shape their learning environment with their hands.

The hand and speech are directly related. If you compare PET scans of verbal language with a map of the neo-cortex, you find that the primary area for speech is the hand, with the secondary area being verbalization. We know that gesturing is essential for fluent speech and gives us the pictures and words we need, even when talking on the telephone. We use our hands to access our thoughts. Children struggling with language are able to finally pick it up when they begin using sign-language. Children in cultures like Japan still do origami daily, and Scandinavian children knit, in order to gain fine motor skills and spatial awareness.

Historically, humans have had an innate urge to increase the efficiency of their communications. Egyptian hieroglyphics was a gorgeous script, but was time-consuming and reserved for inscriptions on metal and stone. When writing on papyrus, they used the cursive hieratic script, a system of joined letters that allowed the scribe's hand to flow freely. Cursive has existed through all times around the world. Virtually every civilization that manage to develop a system of writing, formulated a quickie version that connects the letters. For centuries, the educated, wealthy and refined could be distinguished by their ability to create beautiful flowing letters.

Rudolph Steiner felt that cursive writing was essential for development not only of language and fine motor skills, but for a creative mind because it allows the thoughts and spirit to flow freely. The Waldorf schools in Europe began with cursive writing at approximately 7 years of age, before the carpel bones of the hand are developed enough to do the difficult fine motor activity of printing.

Maria Montessori felt that the hand was the direct link to the mind. Young children were instructed in language arts through the introduction of sandpaper letters which the child traces, while simultaneously saying its phonetic sound. When the pencil was placed in his hand, the child instinctively knew how to accurately reproduce the letter. Cursive writing fits the child's natural instincts. The flow and movement engages the child in language learning, and leads to a sense of accomplishment and confidence.

Children who learn cursive writing have no problem deciphering block printing or words that are the first and last letter in place, with the rest of the letters scrambled. Can you decipher the following?

"Aoccdrnig to rseerach at Cmabrigde Uinervtisy, it deosn't mttaer in what oder the ltteers in a word are, the only iprmoatnt thing is that the frist and lsat ltteer be at the rghit pclae. The rset can be a total mses and you can still raed it wouthit porbelm. This is bcuseae the human mind deos not raed ervey lteter by istlef, but the word as a wlohe."

Researchers have discovered the following regarding cursive writing:

- The hand, our greatest tool, has exquisite versatility and precision
- The ability to manipulate physical objects aligns with the acquisition of speech
- Cursive handwriting unifies hand, eye and attention at a single point in space and time.

- Patients with brain lesions that impair cursive handwriting also struggle to recognize letters by sight.
- Both seeing handwritten and typed letters stimulates activity in the visual cortex, but cursive handwriting also produces activity in the motor cortex.
- Electro-encephalograms show that only the left brain is active when a person prints, while the whole brain is active when writing in cursive.
- Cursive handwriting, more than printing or typing, stimulates intelligence and language fluency. Fluent writing keeps us from truncating our thoughts.
- MRI studies at Indiana and Vanderbilt University found more brain activity when writing versus typing.
- Handwriting increases the brains capacity for keeping and organizing information.
- When kids were asked to write the alphabet from memory, it was the single best predictor of not only spelling but the quality and amount of writing they composed.
- Hand-formed letters, inscribed more deeply in our mind, are building blocks for sturdier mental architectures.
- Cursive writing connects letters, making words. And connecting those words means connecting thoughts.
- The precise geometries that make up handwritten characters, takes years to develop and are so rich that forensic analysts know that no two people have the same script.

- Knowledge of letterforms learned by writing persisted, whereas typed learning dissipated.
- Children rarely produces two identical letters, thus they make up a mental library of the many variations a single letter can take.
- Letter recognition is fundamental to reading, spelling and translating ideas into text or expressing concepts clearly.
- Writing is a mental process - - an ever shifting, feedback interplay between thoughts and knowledge.
- Processes traditionally done with handwriting, like brainstorming mind-mapping and outlining remain clumsy on computers.
- Studies at Vanderbilt University noted that kids with sloppy handwriting score lower on tests, regardless of the content of their ideas.
- There is something special about how a pen rests in the hand and moves across paper as a meditative flow arising from motor and sensory unity. The text also feels somehow more complete, more intimate, and more creative.

"Researchers state that it is not about whether printing, typing or cursive is more important. Learning cursive actually helps a child's ((adult's)) brain develop." Brandon Keim

Many elementary schools have dropped cursive instruction all together as increased testing, Common Core State Standards issued in 2010, and Computers in the classroom take more time and resources. A few states have recently moved to make cursive writing mandatory.

The Common Core states that students must know keyboarding by fifth grade, but doesn't even mention cursive. A large percentage of teachers (85%) never receive training to teach cursive writing. And yet almost half the school day in primary grades is spent writing in workbooks, math tests, quizzes. This carries through to higher grades where part of the ACT and SAT tests are handwritten, with those penning essays in cursive scoring higher than the ones who printed, according to the College Board. Printing is far easier to forge, people still need to sign documents in cursive, and be able to read historical documents like the Constitution.

Bridging the gap with Brain Gym®, Vision Gym, and Hand/Arm Games.

References:
Cabrera, Derek, and Laura Colosi. *The World at our Fingertips.*
    Scientific American Mind, September/October 2010. P. 36-41.
Connolly, Kevin. T*he Psychobiology of the Hand.* New England
    Journal of Medicine, Oct. 25, 2001.

Coventry, Andrea, *The Cursive Writing Debate: Neurological Necessity vs. Standardized Testing.* March 28, 2012.

Common Core Standards for English Language Arts & Literacy in History/Social Studies, Science and Technical Subjects

Goldin-Meadow, Susan. *Hands in the Air, Gestures reveal subconscious knowledge and cement new ideas.* Scientific American Mind, September/October 2010, p. 48-55.

Hensher, Philip. *The Missing Ink: The Lost Art of Handwriting.* Farber and Farber, 2012.

Keim, Brandon. *The Science of Handwriting.* Scientific American Mind. September/October, 2013, p. 54-59.

Lawrence, Star. *Handwriting Is Far from Obsolete, Mind Those P's and Q's.* The Costco Connection. August, 2012.

Magen, Anne, and Valay, Jean-Luc. *Digitizing Literacy: Reflections on the Haptics of Writing.* In. Advance in Haptics. Editing by Mehrdad Hosseini Zadeh. InTech, 2010.

McLean, Leah. *Brain Development Could Suffer as Cursive Writing Fades.* KAALtv.com, February 18, 2013.

McNeill, David. *Gesture and Thought.* University of Chicago Press, 2005.

Palmer, Brian. *Is Cursive Dead, Not on Your Life.* April 29, 2011. http://www.slate.com/id2292588

Richards, Todd., et al. *Functional Magnetic Resonance Imaging Sequential-finger Movement Activation Differentiating Good and Poor Writers.* Journal of Clinical and Experimental Neuropsychology. Vol. 31 (8), November 2009. P 967-983.

Rush, Danielle. *Area Schools Keeping Cursive Writing.* Kokomo Tribune.

Sylwester, Robert. *Are Reading and Writing Innate Skills?* October 2, 2011.

Tenner, Edward. *Handwriting Is a 21st-Century Skill.* The Atlantic, April, 28, 2011.

Tobias, Suzanne Perez. *Cursive Writing Fading from Focus in Schools.* The Wichita Eagle.

Wilson, Frank. *The Hand: How Its Use Shapes the Brain, Language, and Human Culture.* First Vintage Books Edition, 2001.

Zezima, Katie. *The Case for Cursive.* The New York Times, April 27, 2011.

Bibliography

Dennison, Paul E. and Gail E. Dennison. *Brain Gym® Teacher's Edition; The Companion Guide to Brain Gym®: Simple Activities for Whole Brain Learning.* Ventura, Ca, Hearts at Play Inc. 2010.

Dennison, Paul E and Gail E. Dennison. *Brain Gym® 101, Balance for Daily Life.* Ventura, Ca. 2007

Dweck, Carol, Ph.D. *Mindset: The New Psychology of Success.* New York, Random House. 2006.

Hannaford, Carla, Ph.D. The Dominance Factor; *How Knowing Your Dominant Eye, Ear, Brain, Hand & Foot Can Improve Your Learning.* Utah, Great River Books. 1997.

Hannaford, Carla. *Smart Moves; Why Learning Is Not All In Your Head.* Salt Lake City, Utah. Great River Books. 2005.

Krasnic, Toni. *How to Study with Mind Maps: The Concise Learning Method.* Concise Books Publishing. 2012.

The New Lexicon Webster's Dictionary of the English Language, Encyclopedic Edition. Lexicon Publications, Inc. New York. 1988.

http://www.au.reachout.com/what-is-self-talk

http://www.blog.penningtonpublishing.com/study_skills/the-top-nine-tips-to-taking-true-false-tests/

http://www.carleton.ca/lss/wp-content/uploads/TOP10-ShortAnswerExams.pdf

https://www.ccsr.uchicago.edu/sites/default/files/publications/p0e01.pdf questions adapted from a study on pre-service teachers.

http://www.conciselearning.com

http://www.dailyteachingtools.com/tips-for-exam-taking.html

http://www.dictionary.reference.com/browse/achievement by Oxford

http://www.dominican.edu/dominicannews/study-highlights-strategies-for-achieving-goals

http://www.entrepreneur.com/article/237831

http://www.fitness.mercola.com/

http://www.getorganizednow.com/art-students.html

http://www.helpguide.org/articles/sleep/how-to-sleep-better.htm

https://www.howtodothings.com

http://www.mayoclinic.org/healthy-lifestyle/stress-management/in-depth/positive-thinking/art-20043950

http://www.mayoclinic.org/healthy-lifestyle/stress-management/in-depth/social-support/art-2004444

http://www.mentalhealthy.co.uk/news/321-pressure-of-exams-causing-worrying-levels-of-anxiety-in-students.html

How to End Exam Anxiety

The ChildLine National Exam Stress Survey
http://www.netjournals.org/pdf/AERJ/2014/1/13-011. Pdf
    Alvan Ikoku Federal College of Education, Owerri, Imo State, Nigeria
http://www.openpolytechnic.ac.nz/study-with-us/study-resources-for-students/exams/tips-foranswering-exam-questions/different-types-of-exam-questions
http://www.oxyfresh.com/news/ha_nutrition.asp
http://www.psychology.about.com/od/memory/ss/ten-facts-about-memory.htm#step
http://www.psychology.about.com/od/mentalhealth/a/exam-anxiety.htm
http://www.scholarships.com/resources/study-skills/standardized-testing/tips-for-answering-true-false-questions-on-standardized-tests/
https://www.schoolcounselor.org/magazine/blogs/may-june-2010/organized-students-succeess
http://www.students.acu.edu.au/administration_and_enrolment/examinations_and_results/examinations/examination_tips/answering_the_questions/exam_tips_for_short_answer_questions
http://www.testtakingtips.com/test/true.htm-skills/standardized-testing/tips-for-answering-true-false-questions-on-standardized-tests/
http://www.theguardian.com/lifeandstyle/2015/may/10/can-i-do-anything-to-stop-exam-anxiety-exams-fear
http://www.therapists.com/fundamentals/exam-anxiety